Let's Talk 2

Second Edition

Leo Jones

D1604532

CAMBRIDGE
UNIVERSITY PRESS

CAMBRIDGE UNIVERSITY PRESS
Cambridge, New York, Melbourne, Madrid, Cape Town, Singapore, São Paulo, Delhi

Cambridge University Press
32 Avenue of the Americas, New York, NY 10013–2473, USA

www.cambridge.org
Information on this title: www.cambridge.org/9780521692847

First published 2002
Second Edition 2008
4th printing 2009

Printed in Hong Kong, China, by Golden Cup Printing Company Limited

A catalog record for this publication is available from the British Library

Library of Congress Cataloging-in-Publication Data
Jones, Leo, 1943–
 Let's talk 2 / Leo Jones. – 2nd ed.
   p. cm.
 ISBN 978-0-521-69284-7 (student's bk. w/audio CD) – ISBN 978-0-521-69285-4 (teacher's manual) – ISBN 978-0-521-69286-1 (audio CD's)
 1. English language–Textbooks for foreign speakers. I. Title II. Title: Let's talk two.

PE1128.J625 2007
428.2'4–dc22

2007012284

ISBN 978-0-521-69284-7 student's book and self-study audio CD
ISBN 978-0-521-69285-4 teacher's manual and audio CD
ISBN 978-0-521-69286-1 CDs (audio)

Art direction, book design, photo research, and layout services: Adventure House, NYC
Audio production: Full House, NYC

Author's acknowledgments

Many people contributed their hard work, fresh ideas, and helpful advice in the development of
Let's Talk, Second Edition.

The **reviewers** using *Let's Talk* in the following schools and institutes who offered insights and suggestions:
Melissa Heritage, **ELS,** Sanggye Dong, South Korea; Chia-ying Lin, **Chaoyang University of Technology,**
Wufong, Taichung, Taiwan; Wendy Wei-Chien Chiu, **Chinese Culture University,** Taipei, Taiwan; Andrew Kozelka,
David English House, Hiroshima, Japan; Heather Girdhar, **DePaul University,** Chicago, Illinois, U.S.A.; Neil Stapley,
ECC Foreign Language Institute, Tokyo, Japan; Len Carnochan, **E.D.L.S.,** Seoul, South Korea; Peter Frau Céspedes,
Escuela Superior Urbana, Maricao, Puerto Rico; Wanda N. Gonzalez Rivera, **Escuela Superior Vocational,**
Cidra, Puerto Rico; Juan Manuel Espinosa Gutiérrez, **FES Aragón, UNAM,** Mexico City, Mexico; Hee Jeong Park,
Hannam University, Daejon, South Korea; Wesley Dennis, **Hiroshima Shudo University,** Hiroshima, Japan; Patricia
Veciño, **ICANA,** Buenos Aires, Argentina; Haejin Elizabeth Koh and Brian Stokes, **Korea University,** Seoul, South
Korea; Christina Cho Rom Hamm, **LATT,** Seoul, South Korea; Dr. Nicholas Marshall, **Meiji University,** Tokyo, Japan;
Shiow-wen Chen and Vincent Ru-chu Shih, Ph.D., **National Pingtung University of Science and Technology,**
Pingtung, Taiwan; Giles Witton-Davies, **National Taiwan University,** Taipei, Taiwan; Su-Hui Yang, **National
Taiwan University of Science and Technology,** Taipei, Taiwan; Kuei-ping Hsu, **National Tsing Hua University,**
Hsinchu, Taiwan; Jason Moser, **Osaka Shoin Women's University,** Nara, Japan; Meaghan Taylor, **St. Dominic's
Junior High School,** Kaohsiung, Taiwan; Ann McCrory and Barbara Raifsnider, **San Diego Community College,**
San Diego, California, U.S.A.; Adriana Emilia Hernández Aldape, **School Centro de Lenguas Extranjeras,** Tampico,
Mexico; Bill Rago, **Seoul National University of Technology,** Seoul, South Korea; Hsiao-I Hou and Huei-chih
Christine Liu, **Shu-Te University,** Kaohsiung, Taiwan; Ana Helena Simões Venturelli, **Side by Side,** São Paulo, Brazil;
Hilary Sprigler, **Sogang University Language Program,** Seoul, South Korea; Arthur Tu, **Taipei YMCA,** Taipei,
Taiwan; Jia Yuh Shiau, **Takming College,** Taipei, Taiwan; Blanca L. Atayde-Luna, **TecMilenio,** Nuevo Leon, Mexico;
and Mariza Riva de Almeida and Erika Ullmann, **Universidade Federal do Paraná,** Curitiba, Brazil.

The **coordinators** and **teachers** in the following schools who allowed us to observe their classes:
Jason Mark Ham, **Catholic University of Korea,** Gyeonggi-do, South Korea; **David English House,** Hiroshima,
Japan; **ECC College of Foreign Languages,** Osaka, Japan; Deborah Shannon, **Korea University,** Seoul, South
Korea; **Rikkyo University,** Tokyo, Japan; **St. Dominic High School,** Kaohsiung, Taiwan; Ian E. Hughes, **Seoul
National University of Technology,** Seoul, South Korea; and **Taipei YMCA,** Taipei, Taiwan.

The **coordinators** and **teachers** in the following schools who gave us additional suggestions:
Hyun-Joo Lee, **Dong-Duk Women's University,** Seoul, South Korea; Colin McDonald, **Hong-Ik University,** Seoul,
South Korea; Jong-Yurl Yoon, **Kookmin University,** Seoul, South Korea; Shawn Beasom, **Nihon University,** Tokyo,
Japan; Vincent Broderick, **Soai University,** Osaka, Japan; Sun-Young Heo, **Gyeong-In National University of
Education,** Gyeonggi-do, South Korea; and Thomas Brannar, **Yong-In University,** Gyeonggi-do, South Korea.

The **students** and **teachers** in the following schools and institutes who piloted the first edition of *Let's Talk*:
Boston University, Boston, Massachusetts, U.S.A.; **CCBEU,** Belém, Brazil; **Center for English Studies,** New
York City, New York, U.S.A.; **Nagasaki Junior College of Foreign Languages,** Nagasaki, Japan; **Nanzen Junior
College,** Nagoya, Japan; **Southern Illinois University,** Niigata, Japan; **University of Pittsburgh,** Pittsburgh,
Pennsylvania, U.S.A.; **University of Southern California,** Los Angeles, California, U.S.A.

The **editorial** and **production** team:
Janet Battiste, Sylvia P. Bloch, David Bohlke, Karen Brock, Sylvia Dare, Karen Davy, Wesley Dennis, Brigit Dermott,
Jill Freshney, Deborah Goldblatt, Yuri Hara, Louisa Hellegers, Cindee Howard, Lise R. Minovitz, Jason Moring, Sandra
Pike, Bill Preston, Tamar Savir, Jaimie Scanlon, Satoko Shimoyama, Wendi Shin, Kayo Taguchi, Donald Van Metre,
Jenny Wilsen, and Dorothy Zemach.

And Cambridge University Press **staff** and **advisors:**
Harry Ahn, Yumiko Akeba, Gary Anderson, Jim Anderson, Mary Louise Baez, Rita Chen, Kathleen Corley, Kate
Cory-Wright, Elizabeth Fuzikava, Heather Gray, Paul Heacock, Louise Jennewine, Jennifer Kim, Robert Kim, Ken
Kingery, Kareen Kjelstrup, Gareth Knight, John Letcher, João Madureira, Andy Martin, Alejandro J. Martinez, Nigel
McQuitty, Carine Mitchell, John Moorcroft, Mark O'Neil, Catherine Shih, Howard Siegelman, Joseph Siu, Ivan
Sorrentino, Ian Sutherland, Alcione Tavares, Koen Van Landeghem, Richard Walker, and Ellen Zlotnick.

Level 2 Scope and sequence

Working together (pages vi–vii) *Getting started* (pages 2–3)

Units / Lessons	Speaking	Listening	Vocabulary
Unit 1 (pages 4–7) **Getting to know you** 1A What are you like? 1B Breaking the ice	Talking about favorite places and colors; describing personalities; discussing and using icebreakers	A conversation about color and personality; conversations of people meeting for the first time	Adjectives to describe places; colors; expressions to keep a conversation going
Unit 2 (pages 8–11) **Making a good impression** 2A Meeting new people 2B On the phone	Talking about first impressions; role-playing meeting new people and phone conversations; giving and taking messages	An article about first impressions; answering-machine messages	Ways to greet people; phone behavior; expressions for using the phone
Unit 3 (pages 12–15) **Food and cooking** 3A That sounds delicious! 3B Going out to eat	Discussing foods and cooking techniques; talking about restaurant meals; role-playing restaurant conversations	Recipe instructions; conversations in a restaurant	Types of food; cooking techniques; food measurements; international foods; foods on a menu
Unit 4 (pages 16–19) **Weather** 4A What's the weather like? 4B Extreme weather	Talking about weather and seasons; describing extreme weather experiences; giving advice about extreme weather	A weather forecast; advice on what to do in a thunderstorm	Types of weather; adjectives to describe moods; times of day; extreme weather
Units 1–4 Expansion (pages 20–21)			
Unit 5 (pages 22–25) **Working for a living** 5A In the workplace 5B Unusual jobs	Talking about job likes and dislikes; describing job experiences; discussing unusual jobs; talking about what's important in a job	Conversations on the first day of work; interviews with people with unusual jobs	Jobs; workplaces; job features
Unit 6 (pages 26–29) **Leisure time** 6A Hobbies and interests 6B If I had more time, . . .	Describing hobbies and interests; discussing chores; talking about typical activities; making weekend plans	Interviews about leisure activities; a conversation about how people spend their time	Adjectives to describe hobbies; leisure activities; everyday activities and chores
Unit 7 (pages 30–33) **Sports and games** 7A Playing and watching sports 7B How about a game?	Talking about participation in sports; conducting interviews about sports; discussing and playing games	Interviews about sports people play and watch; instructions on how to play games	Sports and games; game categories
Unit 8 (pages 34–37) **Transportation and travel** 8A Getting around town 8B Going places	Discussing traffic and transportation problems; talking about different ways to travel; planning a trip	Interviews about traffic and transportation problems and solutions; descriptions of memorable trips	Ways to travel; traffic and transportation problems; traffic signs
Units 5–8 Expansion (pages 38–39)			

v

Working together

Getting started

A **Work alone** How often do you like to do these things in English conversations? Check (✓) *often*, *sometimes*, or *never*.

In English conversations, I like to	Often	Sometimes	Never
1. ask questions	☐	☐	☐
2. talk about myself	☐	☐	☐
3. talk about my interests	☐	☐	☐
4. plan what to say before I talk	☐	☐	☐
5. talk with people I already know	☐	☐	☐
6. talk with new people	☐	☐	☐
7. talk with native speakers	☐	☐	☐
8. keep quiet and listen to other people talking	☐	☐	☐

B **Pair work** Compare your answers with a partner.

"I often like to ask questions. How about you?"

A **Work alone** What can you say in each situation? Choose a statement or question from the box.

a. **Let's take turns asking the questions.**	e. **Why do you think . . . ?**
b. **Let's compare answers.**	f. **Who wants to go first?**
c. **Whose turn is it?**	g. **Let's work together.**
d. **What should we do now?**	h. **Just a moment, please. I'm not quite ready.**

  _d_   1. You don't know what to do next.

_____ 2. You want to work as a group.

_____ 3. You don't know who wants to go first.

_____ 4. You don't know whose turn it is.

_____ 5. You want to see or hear your partner's answers.

_____ 6. You want to find out someone's opinion.

_____ 7. You aren't ready to begin, and you need more time.

_____ 8. You don't want the same person to always ask the questions.

B **Pair work** Compare your answers with a partner.

Activity 3 **A Group work** Complete this conversation with the statements and questions from Activity 2.

Su Jin: OK, I'm done. Let's ___work together___ . Let's see if we agree on the answers.

Misha: Just _____ . One more minute . . . OK.

Raul: Let's _____ . I think the first picture is number 2 and the second is number 1.

Misha: I agree.

Su Jin: Me, too. What _____ ?

Misha: I'll ask you the questions. You answer them.

Su Jin: Wait! Let's _____ . That way, everyone asks and answers questions.

Misha: Good idea. Who _____ ?

Raul: I'll go first. What are your hobbies?

Su Jin: I like to ride my bike. How about you, Misha?

Misha: I like to sing in the shower. Hey, singing is good for you! Whose _____ ?

Su Jin: I think it's Raul's.

Raul: OK. But first I have another question for Misha. Why _____ . . . ?

B Listen 🎧 Check your answers. Then practice the conversation.

Activity 4 **A Work alone** Write questions about these topics.

	Questions	Answers
Name		
Family		
Friends		
Hobbies		

B Pair work Ask your partner the questions. Write the answers.

C Join another pair Introduce your partner to the other students.

"This is Carmen. She has two brothers and . . ."

Activity 5 **Communication task** Work in groups of three. One of you should look at Task 1 on page 76, another at Task 19 on page 83, and another at Task 21 on page 84. You're going to share ideas about how to improve your English!

1A   *What are you like?*

Activity 1 **A Pair work** Look at these pictures. Where are the people? What are they doing?

"They're at an amusement park. They're laughing and having fun."

B Pair work Describe the places in part A. Which kinds of places do you like the most? the least? Use these words and your own ideas.

busy	crowded	exciting	peaceful	relaxing
calm	dull	noisy	quiet	solitary

"The amusement park is busy and noisy. I like calm, quiet places the most."

C Join another pair Discuss these questions.
- What is your favorite place?
- Why do you like it?
- What does this say about your personality?

"My favorite place is a coffee shop near school. I love to go there with my friends."

4   *Unit 1*

Activity 2

A Work alone Rank these colors from 1 (your favorite) to 9 (your least favorite). Then compare with a partner.

| Purple | Green | White | Pink | Blue | Yellow | Black | Brown | Red |

B Pair work Can you guess what these colors say about your personality? Write the colors next to the statements.

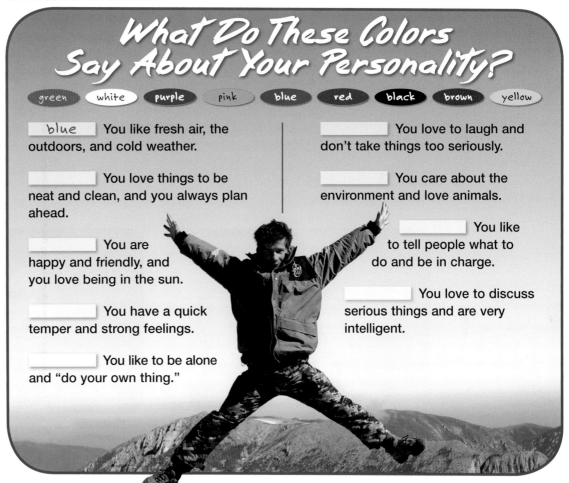

What Do These Colors Say About Your Personality?

green   white   purple   pink   blue   red   black   brown   yellow

blue You like fresh air, the outdoors, and cold weather.

_____ You love things to be neat and clean, and you always plan ahead.

_____ You are happy and friendly, and you love being in the sun.

_____ You have a quick temper and strong feelings.

_____ You like to be alone and "do your own thing."

_____ You love to laugh and don't take things too seriously.

_____ You care about the environment and love animals.

_____ You like to tell people what to do and be in charge.

_____ You love to discuss serious things and are very intelligent.

C Listen 🎧 Did you guess correctly?

D Group work Discuss these questions.
- Is the statement about your favorite color true for you?
- Is the statement about your least favorite color false for you?
- What do you think about this personality analysis? Is it accurate or inaccurate?

"My favorite color is blue. I like fresh air and the outdoors, but I hate cold weather."

Activity 3

Communication task Work in pairs. One of you should look at Task 2 on page 76, and the other at Task 22 on page 84. You're going to ask each other about your habits and personal qualities.

1B Breaking the ice

A Pair work Imagine you want to meet Jenny or Greg. What would you say to "break the ice"?

Jenny

Greg

"I'd say, 'Is anyone sitting here?'"   "You could also say, 'Is this seat taken?'"

B Listen 🎧 Annie is speaking to Jenny, and Tony is speaking to Greg. Check (✔) the icebreakers they use.

Annie
- ☐ Is anyone sitting here?
- ☐ Is this seat taken?
- ☐ Where are you traveling to?

Tony
- ☐ Is the coffee good?
- ☐ How's the coffee here?
- ☐ What are you reading?

C Pair work Discuss these questions.
- Do you usually start conversations or wait for others to talk to you?
- Is it easy or difficult for you to talk to strangers?
- Where are you most likely to start conversations?

"I usually wait for others to talk to me. I guess I'm kind of shy."   "I usually start conversations. I'm a talkative person!"

D Listen 🎧 First, guess Annie's and Tony's questions. Then listen to their conversations. Check your guesses.

Annie's questions

What's _____ ?

Where did _____ ?

What were _____ ?

Who was _____ ?

Jenny's answers

Jenny.

Lincoln High School.

English and geography.

Mrs. Green. She was the best!

Tony's questions

What's _____ ?

What are _____ ?

When will _____ ?

What will _____ ?

Greg's answers

Greg.

A history book.

Next year.

Maybe teach history. I don't know.

Activity 2

A Pair work Check (✓) the icebreakers you'd say to someone you are meeting for the first time. Write an **X** next to the icebreakers you'd never say.

	Someone your age		Someone much older	
	male	female	male	female
How are you doing?	☐	☐	☐	☐
Are you married?	☐	☐	☐	☐
I love your jacket.	☐	☐	☐	☐
What do you do for a living?	☐	☐	☐	☐
We haven't met. My name's . . .	☐	☐	☐	☐

B Join another pair How is your choice of icebreaker different for a male or female? for someone your age or someone much older?

"I wouldn't say 'How are you doing?' to someone much older. It's a little too informal."

Activity 3

A Pair work Imagine you're meeting for the first time. Start a conversation. Use these expressions to keep the conversation going.

Really?   Why is that?   How come?   That's interesting.   What do you mean?

"What are you listening to?"

"Hip-hop. It's my favorite kind of music."

"That's interesting. It's my favorite, too. Who's your favorite singer?"

B Communication task Work in groups of three. One of you should look at Task 3 on page 77, another at Task 20 on page 83, and another at Task 23 on page 85. You're going to find out more about the students in your class.

Self-study For extra grammar, listening, and vocabulary practice, go to pages 94–95.

Meeting new people

Activity 1

A Pair work These people are meeting for the first time. Are they making good first impressions?

"The people in the first picture are making a good first impression."

"I agree. They're smiling, and they look very friendly."

B Pair work Imagine you're meeting someone your age for the first time. Check (✓) the things you usually do. Write an **X** next to the things you never do.

☐ shake hands   ☐ touch the person on the arm

☐ bow   ☐ look at the person directly

☐ hug   ☐ look away from the person

☐ kiss the person on the cheek ☐ offer the person something to drink

☐ smile and say "Hi"   ☐ offer the person something to eat

☐ stand very close   ☐ if sitting, stand up

☐ exchange business cards ☐ if sitting, offer the person a seat

"I guess I usually shake hands. What about you?"

"It depends. I sometimes shake hands, and sometimes I smile and say 'Hi.'"

C Join another pair Compare your answers. Then discuss these questions.

- Are your answers different if the person is older than you? younger than you?
- How do you say good-bye to someone you've just met?

"If the person is older, I always stand up."

"If the person is younger, I usually don't shake hands. I just say 'Hi.'"

A **Pair work** Read this magazine article. Can you guess the missing words?

FIRST IMPRESSIONS

According to psychologists, people form first impressions based on how you _____ , then on how you _____ , and finally on what you say.

The way you look makes up _____ % of a first impression. This includes facial expressions, body language, and eye contact, as well as your clothes and general appearance. A friendly _____ seems to be the most important part of this.

The way you sound makes up _____ % of a first impression and includes how fast or slowly you _____ . People listen to your tone of voice and decide if you sound _____ or unfriendly, interested or _____ , and _____ or sad. What we say — the actual words — counts for only _____ % of the message.

People form first impressions within _____ seconds of meeting you. And first impressions don't change easily. If someone gets the wrong impression of you, it can take a long time to change his or her _____ .

One problem is that in different parts of the world, the same behavior can give people a different impression. In some countries, if you look at the person _____ , it shows you are friendly. In other countries, it can be rude, and it's more polite to _____ away from the person. Standing close to someone and touching the person's arm is normal in some places, but in others it's better to keep your distance. The person may think you're being *too* _____ !

B **Listen** 🎧 Now listen and check your guesses.

C **Pair work** Discuss these questions.

- Which ideas from the article do you agree with? Which do you disagree with?
- Do you think you usually make a good first impression? Why or why not?
- What do you think is most important – how you look, how you sound, or what you say?

A **Pair work** Imagine you're talking to someone you've just met. Which of these things is it OK to do?

answer your phone	look at other people	look through a magazine
make a phone call	send a text message	talk about other people

"It's OK to answer your phone, but it's not OK to make a phone call."

"Do you think so? I think it's kind of rude to answer your phone."

B **Pair work** Role-play meeting for the first time in these situations. Try to make a good first impression!

at a concert   at a party   at a job interview   on the first day of class

"Hi. Great concert, isn't it?"

"Yeah, I really like the music. Are you a friend of Jae Seok's?"

"Yeah. He's in my English class. By the way, I'm Steven. . . ."

2B On the phone

A **Pair work** Look at these pictures. Have these things ever happened to you?

"I was put on hold once. I waited for 30 minutes!"

B **Pair work** What phone behavior bothers you? Ask your partner the questions, and check (✓) the answers.

Does it bother you when someone . . . ?	Yes	Sometimes	No
calls early in the morning	☐	☐	☐
calls late at night	☐	☐	☐
doesn't call back	☐	☐	☐
leaves a long message	☐	☐	☐
puts you on hold	☐	☐	☐
talks too long	☐	☐	☐
talks too loudly	☐	☐	☐
uses call-waiting	☐	☐	☐

C **Join another pair** Discuss these questions.

• Compare your answers from part B. How are they similar?
• How many phone calls do you make each day? How many text messages do you send?
• What do you like the most about using the phone? What do you like the least?

D **Pair work** Imagine both of you want to meet later. Sit back-to-back and role-play a phone call. Use these questions and your own ideas.

Where are you?   What are you doing?
Who are you with?   Where should we meet?

"Hi, this is Allie. Could I speak to Mindy?"

"This is Mindy. Hey, Allie, where are you?"

"I'm still at home. What are you doing?"

Activity 2 **A** **Listen** 🎧 You will hear two answering-machine messages. Complete the top of each message.

❶ For: Bob Smith

From:

Phone number:

....

Message:

❷ For:

From:

Phone number:

....

Message:

B **Listen again** 🎧 Complete the messages.

Activity 3 **A** **Work alone** Imagine you're going to visit a friend. Write your own information.

Name: _____   Cell phone: _____

Arriving on (day): _____   E-mail: _____

Arriving at (time): _____   Place to meet: _____

B **Pair work** Call your partner and ask to speak to the friend. Your partner takes the message. Take turns.

"Hi, this is Ben. Can I speak to Rebecca?"

"Sorry, she's not here. Can I take a message?"

"Yes. Please tell her I'm arriving on . . ."

Name: _____
Arriving on (day): _____
Arriving at (time): _____
Cell phone: _____
E-mail: _____
Place to meet: _____

C **Communication task** Work in pairs. One of you should look at Task 4 on page 77, and the other at Task 24 on page 85. You're going to leave and take more messages.

Self-study For extra grammar, listening, and vocabulary practice, go to pages 96–97.

3A That sounds delicious!

A Pair work Look at these breakfast dishes. Then discuss the questions below.

- Which breakfast looks the best? Why?
- What do you usually have for breakfast? lunch? dinner?
- What's your favorite meal of the day? Why?

"The third breakfast looks the best. I prefer fruit and yogurt in the morning."

B Pair work How many things can you add to the chart?

Meats	Seafood	Fruits	Vegetables	Drinks
lamb	tuna	oranges	carrots	milk

"Can you think of any more meats?"   *"Sure. There's chicken and . . ."*

C Join another pair Compare your lists. Then discuss these questions.

- What things are the same in your lists? What are different?
- What's your favorite in each list? What's your least favorite?
- Which foods can you use these cooking methods with?

| bake | barbecue | boil | broil | fry | grill | steam |

"You can bake cakes and cookies."   *"You can also bake bread and . . ."*

Activity 2 **A Listen** 🎧 Kel is explaining how to make his favorite cookies. How much of each ingredient does he need? Write the quantities.

Ingredients

_125_ grams of butter

_____ tablespoons of water

_____ grams of flour

_____ grams of brown sugar

_____ grams of dried coconut

_____ grams of oatmeal

_____ teaspoon of baking soda

Anzac biscuits

B Listen again 🎧 Complete the instructions.

Instructions

1. First, __heat__ the butter and water in a small pan.
2. Then _____ the melted butter and water into a mixing bowl.
3. Add the other _____ , and mix them together.
4 Drop _____ of the mixture onto a baking tray.
5. Now _____ them at 200°C (400°F) for _____ to _____ minutes.
6. Leave them to _____ on the tray before you eat them.

C Group work Discuss these questions.

- Can you cook? Is there a special dish you can make?
- What are your favorite main dishes?
- What are your favorite desserts? snacks?
- Are there any foods and drinks you have all the time? never have?

"I can cook. I can make cereal with milk."   "That's not cooking!"

Activity 3 **Communication task** Work in groups of four. Two of you should look at Task 5 on page 77, and the other two at Task 25 on page 85. You're going to learn how to make these two dishes.

French crepes

Swiss muesli

A Pair work Imagine you're in a café. Read this menu and decide what to order.

Ida's International Café

Appetizers $8

Sushi: A selection of Japanese-style raw fish on rice.

Dim sum: Steamed or fried Chinese dumplings – meat, seafood, or vegetable.

Main Dishes $12

Bibimbap: Bowl of mixed vegetables, rice, and an egg, mixed with a spicy Korean sauce.

Hamburger and fries: 100% beef hamburger with large order of fries. An American classic.

Fajitas: Mexican-style spicy beef grilled with onions and green peppers. Served with tortillas.

Lamb kebabs: Spicy lamb grilled on sticks. Served with salad and Turkish bread.

Feijoada: Spicy Brazilian stew with beans, meat, and vegetables. Served with rice.

Pad Thai: Stir-fried rice noodles, shrimp, and vegetables. A true taste of Thailand.

> **Special**
> Two people ordering the same main dish only pay for one!

Desserts $4

French crepes: Served with lemon juice and fruit.

Exotic ice-cream sampler: Ginger, coconut, and green tea.

Drinks $3

Iced tea	Carrot juice	Lemonade	Mineral water	Orange juice

"What are you going to have?"

"I'm pretty hungry. I think I'll try the dim sum, the fajitas, and an iced tea."

"I want something light. Maybe I'll just get the sushi and a dessert."

B Pair work Now imagine you each have only $20. Do you want to change your mind?

"If we order the same main dish, we only pay for one."

"OK. Let's get the same main dish. Then we can order an appetizer."

C Join another pair What do you suggest for someone who . . . ?

enjoys spicy food   loves fried food   is on a diet   doesn't eat meat

"For someone who enjoys spicy food, I'd recommend fajitas or . . ."

A **Pair work** These people are in a restaurant. What do you think they're saying? Write your guesses.

B **Listen** 🎧 You will now hear the conversations. Did you guess correctly?

C **Group work** Discuss these questions.
- What kinds of restaurants do you like? What kinds don't you like?
- How often do you go out to eat? Who do you usually go with?
- What's the best meal you've ever had?

A **Group work** Make a menu with dishes from your country or other countries. Include appetizers, main dishes, desserts, and drinks.

B **Group work** Imagine one of you is a waiter or a waitress, and the other two are customers. Role-play a restaurant conversation. Then change roles.

"Are you ready to order?"   "Not yet. I have a question. Is the tuna fresh?"

For extra grammar, listening, and vocabulary practice, go to pages 98–99.

4A What's the weather like?

Activity 1 **A Pair work** Describe the pictures below. What's the weather like in each place? Use the words in the box and your own ideas.

chilly	cool	humid	rainy	stormy	warm
cloudy	foggy	icy	snowy	sunny	windy

San Francisco

Taipei

Geneva

Rio de Janeiro

"It's very foggy in San Francisco."   *"And in Taipei, it looks . . ."*

B Pair work Discuss these questions.

- Would you like to visit any of the places in part A? Is the weather important?
- What's the weather like today where you live?
- What was the weather like last weekend?
- Is your favorite season spring, summer, fall, or winter? Why?

"I'd like to visit Geneva. Snowy weather doesn't bother me."

Activity 2 **A Pair work** How does weather affect your mood? Use the words in the box and your own ideas.

cheerful	depressed	energetic	irritable	lazy	sleepy

"If it's cold outside, I usually feel lazy."

B Pair work Think about next weekend. What do you want to do if it's warm and sunny? cool and rainy? Write three things.

_____   _____

_____   _____

_____   _____

"If it's warm and sunny, I want to go swimming."   *"That sounds good. I think I want to go for a bike ride."*

C Join another pair Compare your ideas. Choose the best things to do.

Activity 3

A Listen 🎧 You will hear the weather forecast for next weekend. Write the weather and temperatures.

Saturday			Sunday		
	Weather	**°C**		**Weather**	**°C**
morning	cloudy		morning		
afternoon			afternoon		
evening			evening		
overnight			overnight		

B Pair work Discuss these questions.

- Is the weather forecast better for Saturday or Sunday?
- What do you think the weather will really be like next weekend?
- Which day last week had the best weather? What did you do?
- What's your favorite type of weather? Why?

Activity 4

Communication task Work in pairs. One of you should look at Task 6 on page 78, and the other at Task 26 on page 86. You're going to find out about the weather in two different cities.

4B *Extreme weather*

A Pair work Look at these pictures. Have you ever been in these types of weather? How did you feel?

| typhoon | blizzard | heat wave |

"I was in a typhoon once. I was terrified!"

B Pair work Which words and phrases in the box go with each kind of weather? Write them in the chart. (More than one answer is possible.)

closed roads	floods	high winds	traffic accidents
drought	frostbite	power losses	wildfires

typhoons	blizzards	heat waves

C Join another pair Compare your ideas. Can you add any more words and phrases to part B?

D Group work Discuss these questions.
- Where are typhoons common? blizzards? heat waves?
- Is there extreme weather where you live? What kind?
- What kinds of weather are the most dangerous? Why?

"Typhoons are common in Asia and . . ."

A **Pair work** What should you do if you are outside during a thunderstorm?
Circle your guesses.

If you're outdoors during a thunderstorm, ...

1. **do / don't** stand under a large tree
2. **do / don't** stand under shorter trees in a forest
3. **do / don't** stand on the top of a hill
4. **do / don't** swim or go out in a boat
5. **do / don't** carry anything made of metal
6. **do / don't** stay away from metal things
7. **do / don't** stay inside a car
8. **do / don't** go inside a big building

B **Listen** You will now hear the first part of an expert's advice. Check
your guesses.

C **Pair work** What should you do if you are inside during a thunderstorm?
Circle your guesses.

If you're indoors during a thunderstorm, ...

1. **do / don't** stand near doors and windows
2. **do / don't** wash dishes
3. **do / don't** take a bath or shower
4. **do / don't** use the telephone
5. **do / don't** disconnect your computer
6. **do / don't** turn off the lights
7. **do / don't** close the curtains
8. **do / don't** go outside

D **Listen** You will now hear the second part of the expert's advice. Check
your guesses.

Group work Discuss these questions.

- Do you remember a day that was particularly hot or cold? What did you do?
- Have you ever been caught in a violent thunderstorm? What did you do?
- Have you ever been caught in a heavy snowstorm? What did you do?

"I remember a day that was particularly hot. I was camping with my friends."

"Really? What did you do?"

"We went swimming in the river."

For extra grammar, listening, and vocabulary practice, go to pages 100–101.

Units 1–4 Expansion

FINISH

What do you want to do if it's sunny tomorrow?

What kind of weather don't you like?

How to play

1 Work in groups. Each player places a token such as a paper clip, a pen cap, or an eraser on **Start**.

2 Take turns. Roll a die, move that number of spaces, and answer the question.

3 Other players can ask follow-up questions.

What do you usually have for breakfast?

What's your favorite meal of the day?

What can you cook well?

Go Back

How many phone calls do you make each day?

Who do you like to talk with on the phone?

What's your favorite icebreaker?

What does your favorite color say about you?

Move Ahead

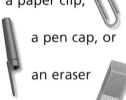

Name three icebreakers.

? Free Question

Describe your personality.

Go Back

What extreme weather have you experienced?

What was the weather like last weekend?

What's your favorite season?

What are your favorite snacks?

What kinds of restaurants do you like?

What do you usually have for lunch?

What's the weather like today?

What can make a bad first impression?

? Free Question

Move Ahead

Go Back

Describe a family member's personality.

How can you make a good first impression?

What do you like about using the phone?

What don't you like about using the phone?

Move Ahead

What's your favorite place?

? Free Question

START

5A In the workplace

Activity 1 **A Pair work** Look at these pictures. Then discuss the questions below.

- What is each person's job?
- What would you like and dislike about each job?
- Do you know anyone with these jobs?

"She's a construction worker."

B Pair work Match the jobs with the workplaces.

Job	Workplace
an accountant	in a hospital
an actor	in a restaurant
an artist	in a school
a chef	on a movie set
a flight attendant	in a store
a lifeguard	in a studio
a nurse	in a university
a professor	in an office
a salesclerk	at the beach
a teacher	on an airplane

"An accountant works in an office."

C Join another pair Discuss these questions.

- Who else works in the workplaces in part B?
- Who has the hardest job? the most interesting job? the best-paying job?
- Which job would you like the most? Why?

"Let's see. A doctor also works in a hospital, and . . ."

A **Pair work** What are the people doing in each picture?

Sally:

Brad:

"What is Sally doing in the first picture?"   *"She's using a computer. Maybe she's . . ."*

B **Listen** 🎧 Sally and Brad are talking to their bosses on the first day of their new jobs. Check (✓) the things they have to do. Put an **X** next to the things they don't have to do.

C **Listen again** 🎧 Complete the sentences.

Sally's working hours are from _____ to _____ .

Her lunch break is from _____ to _____ .

Brad's working hours are from _____ to _____ .

His lunch break is from _____ to _____ .

Activity 3 **Group work** Discuss these questions.

- Have you ever had a job? What did you do? What did you like about it?
- What job do you think you'll have five years from now?
- What job would you most like? Why?
- What do your family members do? What would you like about their jobs?

"Have you ever had a job?"

"Yes, I had a job last summer in a café. I served customers and . . ."

5B *Unusual jobs*

Activity 1 **A Pair work** Look at these pictures. Then discuss the questions below.

dolphin trainer

video-game tester

lumberjack

movie extra

- Do you think the people like their jobs? Why or why not?
- What do you think they do on a typical day?
- Which job would you prefer? Why?

"I think the dolphin trainer really likes her job. She's excited about working with dolphins."

"I agree. I think she has an exciting job."

B Listen You will hear interviews with the people in part A. Check (✓) what they like about their jobs.

Linda dolphin trainer	☐ learning more about animals ☐ performing in front of a crowd	☐ being "friends" with the animals ☐ learning new things every day
Ellen video-game tester	☐ working indoors ☐ playing the latest games	☐ having flexible hours ☐ working alone
Bruce lumberjack	☐ earning good money ☐ working with friends	☐ getting up early ☐ working near home
Andy movie extra	☐ meeting famous people ☐ learning new things	☐ being in front of a camera ☐ having a lot of free time

C Listen again 🎧 What don't they enjoy about their jobs? Take notes.

Linda	*doesn't get much time off*
Ellen	
Bruce	
Andy	

Activity 2

A Pair work What would you like about each job? What would you dislike? Complete the chart.

	What I'd like	What I'd dislike
Actor		
Musician		
Journalist		
Lifeguard		
Politician		
Professional athlete		
Pilot		

B Join another pair Compare your ideas. Then discuss these questions.
- Which three jobs in part A would you like to have the most? Why?
- Which jobs are most popular? Which are least popular?
- What's your ideal job?

"I'd like to be an actor. That would be an interesting job."

"Really? I think I'd be bored."

Activity 3

A Work alone What's important for you in a job? Rank these things from 1 to 9.

_____ a chance to travel   _____ good benefits   _____ flexible hours

_____ a supportive boss   _____ easy work   _____ a chance for promotion

_____ an excellent salary   _____ friendly co-workers   _____ a short commute

B Pair work Compare your answers. Do you have similar ideas?

Activity 4

Communication task Work in groups of three. One of you should look at Task 7 on page 78, another at Task 27 on page 86, and another at Task 37 on page 90. You're going to guess some jobs.

Self-study For extra grammar, listening, and vocabulary practice, go to pages 102–103.

Hobbies and interests

Activity 1 **A** **Pair work** Look at these pictures. Then discuss the questions below.

- What are the people doing?
- Which activities do you regularly do? Which activities do you never do?

"The man in the first picture is lifting weights."   *"The woman in the second picture is . . ."*

B **Listen** 🎧 You will hear interviews with Jason, Emma, and Nick. Write their favorite leisure activities in the chart.

	Favorite leisure activities	What they enjoy about each activity	How long they spend on each activity
Jason	doing yoga		
Emma			
Nick			

C **Listen again** 🎧 What do they enjoy most about each activity? How long do they spend on each thing? Complete the chart.

D **Group work** Discuss these questions.
- Would you rather spend free time with Jason, Emma, or Nick? Why?
- Who wouldn't you like to spend time with? Why not?

"I'd rather spend free time with Nick because I also enjoy . . ."

Activity 2 **A** **Pair work** Describe each hobby below. Use the words in the box and your own ideas.

creative	dull	healthy	rewarding	satisfying	stimulating	time-consuming

shopping

taking photos

knitting

doing puzzles

exercising

playing video games

"I think shopping is relaxing and satisfying."

"Do you think so? I find it dull and time-consuming."

B **Join another pair** What are your favorite hobbies? Why? Use these reasons and your own ideas.

I can do it alone.	It's educational.	I can do it anytime.
I can do it with friends.	It's inexpensive.	I can do it anywhere.

"My favorite hobby is doing puzzles. I can do it alone, and it's relaxing."

"I really like taking photos. I can do it anytime, and it's creative."

C **Group work** Discuss these questions.

- What hobbies did you do as a child but don't do now?
- What new activity would you like to try? Why?
- Do you know anyone with an unusual hobby?

"I collected stamps as a child, but I don't have time for it now."

Activity 3 **Communication task** Work in pairs. One of you should look at Task 8 on page 78, and the other at Task 28 on page 86. You're going to talk about other activities you enjoy.

6B If I had more time, . . .

Activity 1

A Pair work In an average week, how many hours does the average person spend doing these things? Circle your guesses.

Time spent...	Hours	
at home	80	120
in bed	60	90
in the shower	2	4
watching TV	14	28
eating	14	40
cleaning the house	5	10
shopping	6	12
waiting in line	6	12
at work	24	48
in meetings	7	14
in school	6	24
on hobbies	5	10
traveling	3	6
waiting at red lights	½	1

"Do you think the average person spends 80 or 120 hours at home?"

"I'd guess 80 hours. What do you think?"

B Listen Two people are discussing the information in part A. Did you guess correctly? Correct your answers.

C Pair work How much time do you spend doing the things in part A?

"I think I spend more time watching TV, about 20 hours or so."

"I don't spend any time watching TV."

Activity 2

A Work alone Check (✓) the chores you often do. Write an **X** next to the chores you never do.

- ☐ clean my room
- ☐ feed a pet
- ☐ fix broken things
- ☐ do laundry
- ☐ recycle
- ☐ sweep the floor
- ☐ shop for groceries
- ☐ take out the garbage
- ☐ wash dishes

B Pair work Compare your answers. Then discuss these questions.

- Are there any chores you enjoy doing? What are they?
- What chores do you dislike the most? Why?
- What other chores do you do?

"Actually, I enjoy feeding my pet cat and shopping for groceries."

A Work alone Add two activities to the chart that you like to do.

In the past month, how many times did you . . . ?

Activity	You	Your partner
eat out	☐	☐
go for a walk	☐	☐
go dancing	☐	☐
go shopping	☐	☐
go to a café	☐	☐
go to the movies	☐	☐
play a video game	☐	☐
play music	☐	☐
prepare a meal	☐	☐
read a book	☐	☐
read a magazine	☐	☐
visit a museum	☐	☐
watch a DVD	☐	☐
watch TV	☐	☐
	☐	☐
	☐	☐

B Pair work About how many times did you do each activity in the past month? Complete the chart.

"In the past month, how many times did you eat out?"

"Let's see . . . I think I ate out about three times. How about you?"

C Join another pair Compare your charts. Then discuss these questions.
- Who do you think has the most leisure time?
- Who spends their free time most productively? Why?
- If you had more free time, how would you spend it?

A Pair work If you had a free weekend, how would you spend it? Write plans for Saturday and Sunday morning, afternoon, and evening.

"On Saturday morning, I'd like to . . ."

B Join another pair Share your plans. Whose weekend sounds more relaxing? more sociable? more educational? more unusual?

For extra grammar, listening, and vocabulary practice, go to pages 104–105.

Playing and watching sports

Activity 1

A Pair work Look at these pictures. Then discuss the questions below.

- How popular are these sports in your country?
- What other sports are popular in your country?
- What sports do you think are the most exciting? the most boring?
- Are you a sports fan? Why or why not?

"Soccer is very popular. I think it's our most popular sport."

"Actually, I think it's the most popular sport in the world!"

B Listen You will hear the beginning of interviews with Ella, Tony, and Joanne. Answer the questions.

	Ella	Tony	Joanne
1. What sport do you like to watch?	basketball		
2. Do you watch it live or on TV?			
3. How often do you watch it?			

C Listen You will now hear the rest of the interviews. Answer the questions.

	Ella	Tony	Joanne
1. What sport do you like to play?			
2. Do you do it for fun or to win?			
3. Why do you like to do it?			

D Group work Ask one another the questions in parts B and C.

Activity 2 **A Pair work** Add three sports to the chart.

Are you a sports nut?

⬤ aerobics	⬤ judo	⬤ volleyball
⬤ auto racing	⬤ running	⬤ walking
⬤ baseball	⬤ sailing	⬤ weight lifting
⬤ basketball	⬤ skiing	⬤ windsurfing
⬤ cycling	⬤ soccer	⬤ yoga
⬤ golf	⬤ surfing	⬤ _____
⬤ gymnastics	⬤ swimming	⬤ _____
⬤ hiking	⬤ tennis	⬤ _____

"Table tennis is missing. Let's add it to the list."

B Pair work In an average month, how often do you take part in each sport in part A? Number each sport from 0 to 4.

0 = never   **1** = hardly ever   **2** = sometimes   **3** = quite a bit   **4** = all the time

"I do aerobics quite a bit. How about you?"   *"Oh, I hardly ever do aerobics."*

C Pair work Add up your scores. Then go to page 93 to analyze your scores.

D Join another pair Decide which sports in part A are:

competitive sports	indoor sports	relaxing sports	team sports
individual sports	outdoor sports	seasonal sports	year-round sports

"Aerobics is an indoor sport. It's also an individual sport."   *"Actually, I always do it outdoors with friends."*

Activity 3 **Group work** Discuss these questions.

- What's your favorite sport now?
- What was your favorite sport as a child?
- Who's your favorite athlete?
- What's your favorite sports team?
- What's the most exciting sports event you've watched?

"My favorite sport now is definitely surfing."

Activity 2

A Pair work How many games can you think of for each category? Use the games from Activity 1 and your own ideas.

board games	checkers
card games	
computer games	
party games	
puzzles	
tile games	

B Group work Discuss these questions.

- What types of games do you like? What types do you dislike?
- What games would you like to learn?
- Do you ever play word games? Which ones do you know?

"I like board games, like chess and checkers."

"Well, I really like computer games. My favorite is . . ."

Activity 3

A Group work Read these instructions for two word games. Then play one of the games.

Word Associations
One player says a word. The next player says another word that he or she associates with the word.

Example:
A: chess   **B:** play   **C:** theater

If a player can't think of a word (or says a word not associated with the previous word), he or she leaves the game. The last player wins.

Endings and Beginnings
One player says a word. The next player says a word beginning with the letter ending the previous word.

Example:
A: appl<u>e</u>   **B:** <u>e</u>lephan<u>t</u>   **C:** <u>t</u>eache<u>r</u>

If the next player can't think of another word (or uses the wrong letter), he or she leaves the game. The last player wins.

B Communication task Work in groups of three. One of you should look at Task 9 on page 79, another at Task 29 on page 87, and another at Task 41 on page 92. You're going to learn about and play some more word games.

Self-study For extra grammar, listening, and vocabulary practice, go to pages 106–107.

8A *Getting around town*

A **Pair work** Look at these pictures. Then discuss the questions below.

- What's happening in each picture?
- Do these things ever happen to you? How do you feel?
- How do you usually get around town on weekdays? on weekends?

"The man is stuck in a traffic jam. He's sitting in his car with the door open."

B **Pair work** Describe common transportation problems where you live. Use the phrases in the box and your own ideas.

traffic jams	full parking lots	subway or bus overcrowding
not enough taxis	road repairs	slow public transportation

"Slow public transportation is a really big problem."

"I agree. Sometimes it takes me two hours to get to work by bus."

A **Pair work** Ask your partner these questions, and write the answers.

In the past week, how many times have you . . . ?			
traveled by car	_____	ridden a motorbike	_____
taken a bus	_____	traveled by train	_____
taken the subway	_____	taken a taxi	_____
ridden a bike	_____	walked somewhere	_____

B **Join another pair** Compare your answers. Then discuss these questions.

- When was the last time you used each type of transportation?
- Where did you go? How long did it take?
- Why did you travel this way? Did you experience any problems?

"The last time I traveled by car was last weekend."

Activity 3 **A Pair work** Do you know what these signs mean? Check (✓) your guesses. Then turn to page 93 to check the answers.

1
- ☐ Bike lane
- ☐ Watch for bikes

2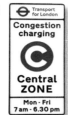
- ☐ No charging
- ☐ Pay to enter downtown

3
- ☐ Pass on right
- ☐ Parking lot

4
- ☐ Buses only
- ☐ Bus parking

5
- ☐ No cars
- ☐ Drive with care

B Listen You will hear five people talk about transportation. Check (✓) the problems.

	Problem		Solution
John	☐ traffic jams	☐ slow drivers	
Anne	☐ too many cars	☐ too little parking	
Carlos	☐ dangerous bikers	☐ dangerous drivers	
Yumiko	☐ no buses	☐ slow buses	
Craig	☐ too much traffic	☐ not enough taxis	

C Listen You will now hear the people suggest solutions. Complete the chart.

D Group work Discuss these questions.
- What traffic and transportation problems are common where you live?
- What solutions could solve the problems?
- What is the worst transportation experience you've ever had?

"Dangerous drivers are a problem where I live."

Activity 4 **A Pair work** What's the best way to get to these places from your school?

| the bus station | the nearest park | the stadium | the zoo |
| the mall | the post office | the train station | your home |

"The best way to get to the bus station is by subway."

"Actually, it's easier and faster to walk. And it's cheaper, too!"

B Pair work Role-play asking for and giving directions to the places in part A.

"Excuse me. Can you tell me how to get to the bus station?"

Activity 5 **Communication task** Work in pairs. One of you should look at Task 10 on page 79, and the other at Task 30 on page 87. You're going to take a transportation quiz.

8B Going places

A **Pair work** Look at these pictures. Then discuss the questions below.

- Have you traveled on a ferry, a high-speed train, or a plane? What was it like?
- What types of transportation would you like to try? Why?
- Do you prefer to go to places quickly or take your time? Why?
- Do you prefer to go to places cheaply or in comfort? Why?

B **Listen** 🎧 Three people are talking about memorable trips. Complete the chart.

	Alice	Rick	Nancy
1. How did they travel?	by train		
2. Why did they travel this way?			
3. How long did it take?			
4. What did they enjoy the most?			

C **Listen again** 🎧 Did anything go wrong on their trips? Complete the sentences.

Alice jumped off _____ and left _____ .

Rick decided to go _____ and got _____ .

Nancy had _____ – _____ went wrong.

D **Pair work** Discuss these questions.

- Which trip do you think you'd enjoy the most? Why?
- Has anything ever gone wrong on a trip? What happened?

"I'd enjoy Alice's trip because I love to travel by train. I don't think I'd enjoy . . ."

A Work alone Complete the chart below with these phrases or your own ideas.

| by airplane | by bike | by boat | by bus | by car | by train | on foot |

What's the best way to travel between . . . ?	Fastest	Cheapest
the largest city and the second largest city where you live		
where you live and a famous mountain		
where you live and the best national park		
where you live and your favorite weekend getaway		
where you live and New York City		
where you live and Antarctica		

B Group work Share your answers.

"The fastest way to travel between . . . and . . . is by train."

"Isn't it faster to go by car?"

"I don't think so. There are often traffic jams and . . ."

Activity 3 **A Pair work** Plan a one-week trip to five different places in your country. Draw a map showing your route. What types of transportation will you use? What activities will you do?

"Let's go to a national park."

"Good idea. But let's do that at the end. First, we should go to . . ."

B Join another pair Explain your travel plans. Which trip sounds better?

Self-study For extra grammar, listening, and vocabulary practice, go to pages 108–109.

Units 5–8 Expansion

How to play

1 Work in groups. Each player places a token such as a paper clip, a pen cap, or an eraser on **Start**.

2 Take turns. Roll a die, move that number of spaces, and say at least one sentence about the topic.

3 Other players can ask follow-up questions.

Start

a job you'd like

a job you wouldn't like

Free Question

your favorite athlete

a sports team you like

a sport you like to watch

Finish

LET'S

a sport you'd like to try

Free Question

a type of transportation you avoid

popular sports in your country

how you like to spend your weekends

how you usually spend your evenings

a friend's or a family member's job

Free Question

what's important to you in a job

an interesting place to work

a game you don't like to play

a game you like to play

a transportation problem where you live

what you enjoy about being a student

TALK ABOUT...

how you prefer to travel

if you'd like to be an actor

a trip you'd like to take

the best way to get home from class

a bad transportation experience

leisure activities you do regularly

Free Question

a hobby you did as a child

an activity you'd like to try

how you spend your free time

A great vacation

Activity 1 **A** **Pair work** Look at what these people did on their vacations. Which vacations look fun? Which don't look fun?

"The camping trip looks fun. It's great to sleep outdoors."   *"I don't think I agree."*

_____ _____ _____

B **Listen** 🎧 Julia, Charlie, and Michael are describing their vacations. Write the name of each person under the correct picture.

C **Listen again** 🎧 Who is describing his or her vacation? Check (✓) the correct boxes.

Who . . . ?	Julia	Charlie	Michael
enjoyed watching the stars	☐	☐	☐
expected to be bored, but wasn't	☐	☐	☐
went to the zoo	☐	☐	☐
got wet and scared	☐	☐	☐
missed his or her friends	☐	☐	☐
went to the opera	☐	☐	☐
thinks the country is too quiet	☐	☐	☐
wishes he or she had planned better	☐	☐	☐
walked over 100 miles	☐	☐	☐

D Pair work Discuss these questions.

- Have you had a vacation like Julia's, Charlie's, or Michael's? What happened?
- What did you do on your last vacation?
- What's the best vacation you've ever had?

> *"Have you had a vacation like Charlie's?"*

> *"I sure have! Last summer, my cousin visited my hometown, and . . ."*

Activity 2 **A Group work** Look at these vacation pictures. Then discuss the questions below.

- What are the people doing? Where do you think they are?
- Imagine that you can take one of these vacations. Which would you choose? Why?

B Group work Describe your perfect vacation. Discuss these questions.

- Where would you go?
- Who would you go with?
- How long would you stay there?
- What would you do there?

> *"I'd go to England and Ireland with my friend Ling."*

C Communication task Work in pairs. One of you should look at Task 11 on page 79, and the other at Task 31 on page 87. You're going to look at more vacation pictures.

9B World travel

Activity 1 **A** **Pair work** Describe these pictures. Use the words in the box and your own ideas.

beach
canyon
cliffs
coast
desert
forest
hills
lake
mountains
rocks
skyscrapers
wildlife

"In the first picture, there are some beautiful mountains and . . ."

B **Pair work** Guess which country the pictures show. Then check your answer on page 93.

"I'm not sure, but I think the country is . . ."

C **Join another pair** Discuss these questions.

- Are any places where you live similar to the places in part A?
- Have you ever visited another country? What did or didn't you like about it?
- If you could visit any country, where would you go? Why?

"We have some high mountains in the north, and there are beaches . . ."

A **Pair work** Sally and Harry just returned from their vacations. Can you guess the country each person visited?

Sally's vacation

Harry's vacation

"I think Sally visited . . ."

B **Listen** Sally and Harry are discussing their vacations. Answer the questions.

	Sally	Harry
1. What season was it?	fall	
2. What was the weather like?		
3. What did he or she enjoy the most?		
4. What was disappointing?		
5. What souvenirs did he or she buy?		
6. Who did he or she travel with?		
7. What country did he or she visit?		

C **Group work** Discuss these questions.

- Which country from part B would you prefer to visit? Why?
- What are the most popular tourist attractions where you live?
- Would you recommend these attractions? Why or why not?
- What three things would you tell a tourist visiting your country to do or see?

"I'd prefer to visit . . . because . . ."

 For extra grammar, listening, and vocabulary practice, go to pages 110–111.

10A I want one of those!

A Work alone What are these gadgets? Match the names with the pictures.

> a. a cell phone
> b. an MP3 player
> c. a laptop computer
> d. an electronic dictionary
> e. a PDA (personal digital assistant)
> f. a GPS (global positioning system) device

B Pair work Describe how you can use the things in part A. Use the phrases in the box and your own ideas.

check e-mail	listen to music	record appointments	store music
find definitions	make calculations	send text messages	translate words
find directions	make phone calls	store addresses	write letters

"You can use a cell phone to make phone calls."   *"You can also use it to send messages."*

C Join another pair Discuss these questions.

- Which gadgets in part A do you own?
- How often do you use them?
- What do you use them for?

"I talk on my cell phone two or three times a day."

"I often use mine to take pictures. I like to send them to my friends."

7B How about a game?

Activity 1 **A Pair work** Look at these games. Then discuss the questions below.

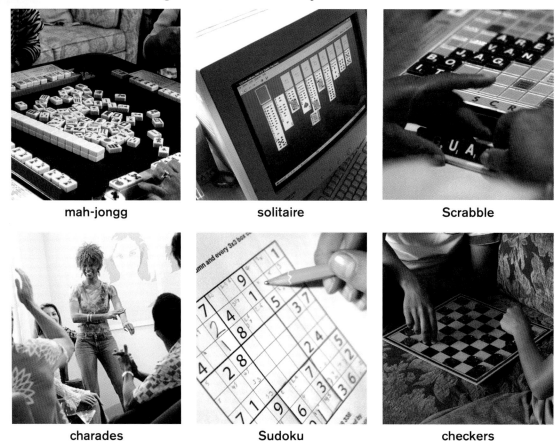

mah-jongg   solitaire   Scrabble

charades   Sudoku   checkers

- Which games have you played?
- Which games did you enjoy the most?
- Which games do you play regularly? from time to time?

"I played mah-jongg once, but I didn't enjoy it."

B Listen 🎧 Three people are talking about their favorite games from part A.
Answer the questions.

	Terry	Lisa	Claudio
1. How many people can play?	one		
2. What equipment do you need?			
3. Does the game involve luck or skill?			
4. How long does a game last?			

C Pair work Can you guess the games they described?

"I think Terry described . . ."

Activity 2

A Work alone How important are these things in your life? Mark them very important (✓✓), somewhat important (✓), or not very important (X).

____ an alarm clock   ____ a DVD player
____ a camera   ____ a microwave oven
____ a CD player   ____ a remote control
____ a dishwasher   ____ a TV

B Pair work Compare your answers. Give reasons.

"An alarm clock is very important in my life. It's hard for me to wake up in the morning!"

Activity 3

A Listen 🎧 Two people are shopping for electronic products. Check (✓) the features.

Portable DVD player

- ☐ 3-year warranty
- ☐ long battery life
- ☐ well-known brand
- ☐ lightweight
- ☐ TV tuner included
- ☐ anti-shock feature
- ☐ big screen
- ☐ two sets of headphones

Camcorder

- ☐ 50 percent discount
- ☐ easy to use
- ☐ image stabilizer
- ☐ takes good still photos
- ☐ compact design
- ☐ records to hard drive
- ☐ records to DVD
- ☐ remote control

B Pair work What features do you think are important for these products?

a camera   a cell phone   a laptop computer   an MP3 player   a TV

"A camera has to be lightweight and easy to use. It should also be ..."

"I don't really agree. A camera doesn't have to be ..."

C Group work Think about the products in part B. Discuss these questions.

- What new features do the products have nowadays?
- Are the latest products all improvements over the older versions?
- Do you have any of the products? Is there anything you don't like about them?

"The latest cameras have ..."

10B Great ideas?

Activity 1 **Pair work** Can you identify these things? Match the names with the pictures. Then discuss the questions below.

a. chopsticks
b. a highlighter
c. a key
d. a magnifying glass
e. a paper clip
f. rubber bands
g. scissors
h. shoelaces
i. a straw
j. a toothbrush

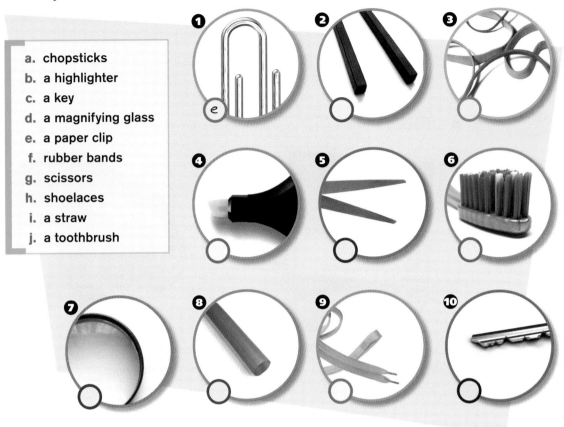

- Which things do you use a lot? Which do you never use?
- Which thing is the most useful? Why?
- Is there anything you can't do without?

"I use a key all the time. I never use . . ."

Activity 2 **A Pair work** Look at these products you can buy. What do you think they're used for? How much do you think they cost?

Pencorder

Safe-T-Man

TV Remote Control Locator

"I think the Pencorder is used for . . ."

B Listen 🎧 You will hear a TV show about the products from part A. Check (✓) the main function of each product.

	Main function	One important feature	Price
Pencorder	☐ records messages ☐ makes phone calls ☐ writes messages		
Safe-T-Man	☐ answers the phone ☐ keeps people safe ☐ catches robbers		
TV Remote Control Locator	☐ changes TV channels ☐ finds TV remotes ☐ cleans TV remotes		

C Listen again 🎧 Complete the chart.

D Group work Discuss these questions.
- Which product sounds the most useful? the least useful?
- What kind of person might use each product?
- Have you bought any products recently? Were you happy with them?

"The TV Remote Control Locator sounds the most useful. I'm always losing the remote."

"I think that's the least useful. What if you lose the TV Remote Control Locator?"

E Communication task Work in pairs. One of you should look at Task 12 on page 80, and the other at Task 32 on page 88. You're going to learn about two more products.

Activity 3

A Pair work What new invention would be really useful? Draw a picture of your invention. Then discuss these questions.
- What's it called?
- What does it do?
- How does it work?
- How much should it cost?
- Who might buy it?

A Robot Maid to clean my room

A Perfect Pen for perfect homework

Super Glasses to see through walls

B Join another pair Now explain your invention, and answer any questions.

"Our invention is called the Perfect Pen. It never makes mistakes, and . . ."

Self-study For extra grammar, listening, and vocabulary practice, go to pages 112–113.

11A Animals and nature

Activity 1 **Pair work** Look at these pictures. Then discuss the questions below.

- Do you enjoy visiting zoos? Why or why not?
- Have you ever visited a botanical garden or a nature park? What was it like?
- Do you like plants or flowers? Do you have any in your home?

"I love visiting zoos. It's fun to see different wild animals."

Activity 2 **A Pair work** How many different animals can you think of? Write them in the chart.

Mammals	Birds	Insects	Fish	Reptiles
gorilla	duck	ant	shark	crocodile
monkey	parrot	mosquito	tuna	snake

B Join another pair Compare your charts. Then discuss these questions.

- Which of these animals have you seen? Where?
- What are the animals like? Are they dangerous? cute? ugly?
- Are any of these animals endangered?
- Which animals can be pets?
- What are your favorite animals? Why?

"I've never seen a gorilla, but I've seen lots of monkeys at the zoo."

C Communication task Work in groups of four. Two of you should look at Task 13 on page 80, and the other two at Task 33 on page 88. You're going to talk about pets.

A Pair work What do you know about meerkats and pandas? Read the questions below, and make guesses.

meerkats

pandas

"Do you know where meerkats live?"

"I'm not sure where they live. But I think they eat . . ."

	Meerkats	Pandas
1. Where do they usually live?	the southern part of Africa	
2. What do they usually eat?		
3. What do they do when not eating?		
4. How many babies do they have?		
5. How long do they live in the wild?		
6. How long do they live in captivity?		
7. Are they endangered?		

B Listen A zookeeper is talking about meerkats and pandas. Answer the questions in part A. Did you guess correctly?

C Group work Discuss these questions.

- Are you concerned about animals becoming extinct? Why or why not?
- What animals in your country are endangered?
- How can we protect endangered species?

"I'm very concerned. Once an animal becomes extinct, it's gone forever."

"I'm not that concerned. I think . . ."

Activity 1 **Pair work** Look at these pictures. Then discuss the questions below.

deforestation   water pollution   air pollution

- Do you have these environmental problems where you live?
- What other environmental problems do you have?

"Deforestation isn't a big problem here."

"It's not a problem in this city, but it's a problem in . . ."

Activity 2 **A** **Pair work** How concerned are you about the environment? Answer the questions. Number each item from 0 to 4. Then interview your partner, and mark the answers.

0 = never   **1** = hardly ever   **2** = sometimes   **3** = often   **4** = always

Do you...?	You	Your partner
recycle paper, glass, cans, and plastic	☐	☐
reuse products such as plastic bags and paper	☐	☐
repair items instead of throwing them away	☐	☐
avoid buying over-packaged products	☐	☐
pick up other people's litter	☐	☐
use public transportation for long distances	☐	☐
walk or use a bike for short distances	☐	☐
turn off the lights when you leave a room	☐	☐
use low-energy lightbulbs	☐	☐
make sure the heat isn't turned up too high in the winter	☐	☐
turn the air conditioning down in the summer	☐	☐
avoid using more water than you need	☐	☐

B **Pair work** Add up your scores. Then go to page 93 to analyze your scores.

C Join another pair Discuss these questions.

- Which things in the questionnaire help the environment the most? Why?
- What other things can you do to help the environment?
- Are there laws to protect the environment where you live? What are they?

Activity 3 **A Listen** 🎧 A park ranger is describing past environmental problems at Hanauma Bay Nature Preserve in Hawaii. Check (✔) the reasons for each problem.

Problem	Reasons	
1. Too few fish	☐ people catching fish ☐ disease	☐ people eating fish ☐ water pollution
2. Too many fish	☐ people catching fish ☐ too few predators	☐ people overfeeding fish ☐ too many plants
3. Too many visitors	☐ beautiful preserve ☐ free fish	☐ great swimming ☐ good restaurants

B Listen again 🎧 How did they solve the problems? Complete the sentences.

Problem 1: They passed a law against _____ that also stopped people from taking away shells, rocks, and coral as _____ .

Problem 2: They passed a law against _____ the fish and moved the _____ farther from the ocean.

Problem 3: They close the preserve every _____ and don't allow new visitors if the _____ is full.

C Group work Can you think of any environmental problems where you live? What solutions can you suggest?

"Air pollution is a big problem in City Park. One reason is there are too many cars."

"Maybe they can pass a law. They should only allow cars . . ."

Self-study For extra grammar, listening, and vocabulary practice, go to pages 114–115.

12A Good news!

Activity 1 **A Pair work** Look at these pictures from the TV news. What do you think each story is about? Use the words in the box and your own ideas.

| competition | lost | prize | reunited | sign | waves |
| flood | ocean | rescue | rowboat | trophy | winner |

"I think the woman is the boy's mother. She looks happy. Maybe the boy was lost."

"Maybe. Can you read the sign behind them?"

B Listen You will hear four news reports. Complete the summaries.

❶ **B**rennan Hawkins, 11, got lost in the mountains of Utah while camping with the Boy Scouts. Over _____ people quickly joined the search after the family created a Web site asking for _____ . He was found _____ days later, hungry and thirsty, but fine.

❷ **O**llie Hicks, 23, is the _____ person to row across the Atlantic Ocean from west to east. His time of _____ days is also the _____ . On the beach to meet him on arrival in Cornwall, England, was his old _____ friend, Prince William.

52 *Unit 12*

3 The number one speller in the United States is Katharine Close, 13, from Spring Lake, New Jersey. She won the Scripps National [ ] Bee on her [ ] attempt. She won more than $[ ] in cash and prizes. She practices her spelling every [ ] .

4 There were bad [ ] when the Red [ ] burst its banks in Grand Forks, North Dakota. One family lost their dog when they abandoned their home. [ ] days later, Scott Frederick heard barking from the family's [ ] . He saved the dog in his boat.

C Group work Discuss these questions.

- Which story had the happiest ending?
- Which story did you like the best?
- Have you read or heard about any similar stories?

Activity 2 **A Pair work** Choose one picture. Use the questions below to make a story.

- Who are the people?
- What happened?
- What happened before?
- What happened later?

B Join another pair Tell your story. Whose story is more interesting?

12B Did you hear about . . . ?

A **Work alone** Complete this news survey.

News and Current Events

1. How much time do you spend learning about the news every day?

☐ 0–5 minutes ☐ 10–20 minutes

☐ 5–10 minutes ☐ more than 20 minutes

2. How often do you get your news from these sources?
Write *O* (often), *S* (sometimes), or *N* (never).

☐ friends ☐ radio ☐ Internet ☐ local newspaper

☐ family ☐ TV ☐ magazine ☐ national newspaper

3. Which sections do you usually read in a newspaper? Which do you ignore? Write *R* (read) or *I* (ignore).

☐ world news ☐ weather ☐ business

☐ national news ☐ sports ☐ TV or movie listings

☐ local news ☐ comics ☐ arts and leisure

☐ classifieds ☐ science ☐ other _____

B **Pair work** Compare your answers. Then discuss these questions.

- How are you and your partner similar? How are you different?
- If you read a newspaper, which section do you read first?
- Is it important for you to learn about current events? Why or why not?
- What news sources do you trust the most? the least?

"You spend more time learning about the news than me. I only spend . . ."

"We both get some of our news from . . ."

Activity 2 **A** **Pair work** What were the five most important stories from the past year? Make a list.

B **Join another pair** Compare your lists. Try to agree on a single list.

"We think the election was an important story."

"Really? We think . . . was more important because . . ."

C **Group work** Discuss these questions.

- Which story from the past year do you think got too much attention? Why?
- What is this week's "big" story? Why is it important?

A Pair work Read these news articles. Try to guess the missing words.

Dog Helps Burglar

Bruce Green of Brisbane, Australia, trained his dog to [____] the front door from inside the house. The dog learned to [____] up and pull the handle down with its paws. But last weekend, the house was [____].

A burglar stole $100 in [____] and a computer from the house. Because there was no sign of a break-in, the [____] are sure that the dog opened the door.

Time Is Money

Mary Brown of Chicago was very [____] when her ex-husband remarried. She still had the [____] to his apartment. While he and his new wife were on their [____], she went to the apartment and called the Speaking Clock in London for the [____]. She didn't hang up the phone.

When the couple returned two weeks later, the phone was still on. The phone bill was $[____].

Clever Octopus

Frieda, an octopus at the Munich Zoo in Germany, has learned how to open jars of her favorite [____] snacks. More and more [____] are coming to the zoo to watch her open jars of shrimp and clams.

"All we did was open some jars [____] where she could see us," says a zoo attendant. "Frieda learned [____] and now opens all the jars herself. But she refuses to open [____] jars."

B Listen 🎧 Two people are talking about the news stories. Write the missing words. Did you guess any words correctly?

C Group work Discuss these questions.
- Which story did you like the best? Why?
- Do you believe everything you read? Why or why not?

"I liked the story about the . . . the best."

Communication task Work in groups of three. One of you should look at Task 14 on page 81, another at Task 34 on page 89, and another at Task 39 on page 91. You're going to read and hear about more news stories.

For extra grammar, listening, and vocabulary practice, go to pages 116–117.

Units 9–12 Expansion

FINISH

How interested are you in current events?

What kind of news stories do you dislike?

How to play

1 Work in groups. Each player places a token such as a paper clip, a pen cap, or an eraser on **Start**.

2 Take turns. Roll a  die, move that number of spaces, and answer the question.

3 Other players can ask follow-up questions.

What's your favorite animal?

What pet would you like to have?

What's the world's biggest environmental problem?

Go Back

What new invention would be really useful?

What gadget have you bought that you were happy with?

Where's the best place to live in your country?

What country would you like to visit?

Move Ahead

What did you do on your last vacation?

?
Free Question

What short trip would you like to take?

Go Back

What news source do you trust the most?

Where do you get your news?

What local stories are in the news this week?

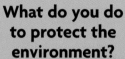
What do you do to protect the environment?

How concerned are you about the environment?

What law would help protect the environment?

What was the biggest news story last year?

What everyday things can't you live without?

? Free Question

Move Ahead

Go Back

Describe a "perfect" weekend.

What electronic gadgets do you own?

What electronic gadgets would you like to have?

What cell phone features are most important?

Move Ahead

What's the best vacation you've ever had?

? Free Question

START

13A The best place to live

A **Pair work** Ask your partner the questions in the survey, and check (✔) the responses.

Which do you prefer, . . . ?

⃝ being indoors	or	⃝ being outdoors
⃝ staying busy	or	⃝ being relaxed
⃝ being in crowded places	or	⃝ being in quiet places
⃝ going to nightclubs	or	⃝ going camping
⃝ taking a subway or bus	or	⃝ walking or riding a bike
⃝ letting an alarm clock wake you up	or	⃝ letting the sun wake you up
⃝ eating in a restaurant	or	⃝ having a picnic
⃝ listening to traffic noise	or	⃝ listening to birds

B **Pair work** Is your partner more of a city person or a country person? Give reasons.

"You prefer being outdoors, so I think you're more of a country person."

"Not really. I like being outdoors – but in the city!"

C **Pair work** What are some advantages of living in a city? living in a small town? Write them in the chart.

Living in a city	Living in a small town
more kinds of entertainment	more fresh air

D **Join another pair** Compare your charts. Then discuss these questions.

- What can you find in a city but not in a small town? a small town but not a city?
- What are some disadvantages of living in a city? a small town?
- Where do you live now? Have you always lived there?
- What do you like about where you live? What don't you like?

"You can find a subway in the city but not in a small town."

Activity 2 **A** **Listen** 🎧 Peter, Angie, and Jeff are talking about cities they used to live in. Check (✓) the name of each city.

Peter

Jeff

☐ Taipei   ☐ San Juan   ☐ Casablanca
☐ Hong Kong   ☐ Mexico City   ☐ Cairo
☐ Singapore   ☐ Rio de Janeiro   ☐ Istanbul

B **Listen again** 🎧 What do they say about the cities? Complete the chart.

	Peter	Angie	Jeff
Feelings on arrival	*excited*		
Best ways to get around			
Best things to see			
Things they miss			

C **Group work** Discuss these questions.

- What information about the cities surprised you?
- Which of these cities would you prefer to live in? Why?
- Which city in the world would you most like to visit? Why?

"I was surprised that it's warm all year-round in Hong Kong."

Activity 3 **Communication task** Work in pairs. One of you should look at Task 15 on page 81, and the other at Task 35 on page 89. You're going to talk about two other cities.

13B Better safe than sorry!

Activity 1

A Work alone How often do you do these things? Write *O* (often), *S* (sometimes), or *N* (never).

____ I go out alone at night.

____ I make eye contact with strangers.

____ I talk to strangers.

____ I use public transportation late at night.

____ I carry a large amount of cash.

____ I wear an expensive watch or jewelry at night.

____ I walk on dark, lonely streets.

____ I leave my door unlocked when I'm home.

____ I leave my car doors unlocked while driving.

B Pair work Compare your answers. Do you do the same things? Do you feel safe doing them?

"I go out alone at night. I guess I feel safe."

"I go out at night, too, but always with someone else."

C Join another pair Read these safety tips. Then discuss the questions below.

Safety Tips

Always tell someone where you're going. Then call after you arrive.

Keep your bags near you at all times.

If you need directions, ask a police officer.

Take taxis instead of buses late at night.

Keep your user ID and passwords secret.

Never let strangers into your home.

Keep your wallet in an inside pocket.

- Which tips do you think give the best advice?
- Do you think any tips are too cautious? Why?
- What other tips can you add?
- What might happen if you don't follow the tips?

"I think the best advice is to take taxis instead of buses at night."

"I'm not so sure I agree. I think buses are safer."

A Pair work Look at these pictures of crimes. What do you think happened?

The Baltimore Burglar

The Chicago Shoplifter

The Boston Bank Robber

The Minneapolis Mugger

"I think the Baltimore Burglar stole some things and . . ."

B Listen You will hear about the crimes in part A. Complete the summaries.

1. The Baltimore Burglar ___broke___ into an apartment in the city. He couldn't [____] out. He called his wife for [____], but her cell phone was turned off. He waited for the owner for [____] days. Then he called the police and was [____].

2. [____] were chasing the Chicago Shoplifter. She climbed over a six-foot [____] and jumped into the yard of the local [____]. The guards [____] the police. They found ten stolen [____] in her pocket.

3. The Boston Bank Robber was trying to cut open a bank [____]. After several hours, she cut a small [____] and put her [____] inside. The bank [____] returned, and she was arrested. Then she found out the door wasn't [____].

4. The Minneapolis Mugger tried to take two [____]-year-old women's [____]. The women were good at [____] and threw him to the ground. Then they [____] him in the trunk of his car and drove to the [____] station.

C Group work Discuss these questions.

*   Which criminal was the unluckiest? the dumbest?
*   Have you heard any other stories about unlucky or dumb criminals?

"I think the Minneapolis Mugger was the unluckiest because . . ."

Self-study For extra grammar, listening, and vocabulary practice, go to pages 118–119.

14A What do you enjoy?

Activity 1 **A Work alone** Which activities do you enjoy the most? Rank them from 1 (most enjoyable) to 6 (least enjoyable).

B Pair work Compare your answers. Then discuss these questions.

- Which activities do you enjoy the most? Is there anything neither of you likes?
- Which activities do you like to do alone? with your friends? with your family?
- What other things do you like to do?

"Both of us like to play video games and watch TV. Neither of us enjoys . . ."

Activity 2 **A Listen** 🎧 Someone is changing radio stations. Grade each piece of music from A to F.

1. _____
2. _____
3. _____
4. _____
5. _____

A = Great! I love this kind of music.
B = This music is pretty good.
C = It's OK, but it's not my favorite.
D = I'm not crazy about it.
F = I can't stand this kind of music.

B Listen again 🎧 Match the pieces of music with their types.

1. _____ a. country and western
2. _____ b. jazz
3. _____ c. classical
4. _____ d. easy listening
5. _____ e. heavy metal

C Group work Discuss these questions.

- What are your favorite kinds of music?
- Who are your favorite male singers? female singers?
- What's your favorite band?
- Do you have a favorite song? Why do you like it?

Activity 3

A Listen 🎧 Three people are choosing a DVD to watch tonight. Match the actors with their characters.

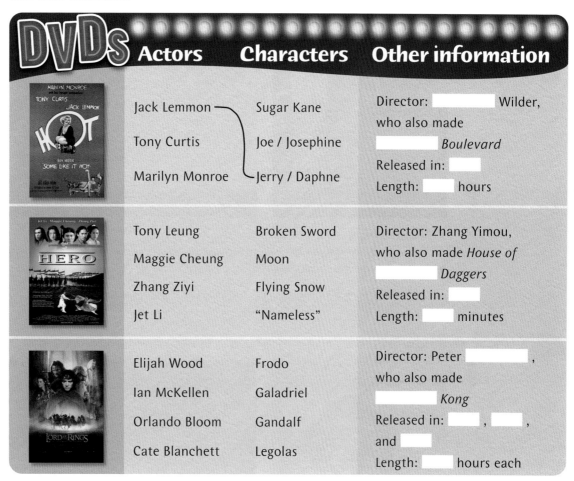

DVDs	Actors	Characters	Other information
Some Like It Hot	Jack Lemmon Tony Curtis Marilyn Monroe	Sugar Kane Joe / Josephine Jerry / Daphne	Director: _____ Wilder, who also made _____ Boulevard Released in: _____ Length: _____ hours
Hero	Tony Leung Maggie Cheung Zhang Ziyi Jet Li	Broken Sword Moon Flying Snow "Nameless"	Director: Zhang Yimou, who also made *House of* _____ *Daggers* Released in: _____ Length: _____ minutes
Lord of the Rings	Elijah Wood Ian McKellen Orlando Bloom Cate Blanchett	Frodo Galadriel Gandalf Legolas	Director: Peter _____, who also made _____ Kong Released in: _____, _____, and _____ Length: _____ hours each

B Listen again 🎧 Complete the other information.

C Group work Discuss these questions.

- What's your favorite movie? What do you like about it?
- What kinds of movies do you like? What kinds don't you like?
- Do you prefer to watch movies on DVD or in a theater? Why?
- Which actors do you like? Which of their movies would you recommend?

"My favorite movie is . . . . It has great special effects, the story is interesting, and . . ."

D Group work Think of a movie you've seen. What's it about? Would you recommend it?

" . . . is a movie about two people who fall in love. At first, they're really happy."

"What happens? Do they break up?"

14B But is it art?

Activity 1 **Pair work** Look at these pictures. Then discuss the questions below.

- Which picture is the most artistic? the least artistic? Why?
- Which picture do you like the most? the least?
- What do you think the people in the pictures are like?

"This one is the most artistic."   *"I don't think so. Anyone can take a photo like that."*

Activity 2 **A Pair work** Look at these self-portraits. Then discuss the questions below.

| Vincent van Gogh | Frida Kahlo | Pablo Picasso |

- Can you guess how old each artist is in the paintings?
- Which painting do you like the most? Why?
- What do you know about these artists?

"I think Vincent van Gogh is about . . ."

B Listen 🎧 Kevin and Lucy are looking at the self-portraits in an art museum. Complete the first two columns of the chart.

	Age self-portrait was painted	Age the artist died	Number of paintings	Highest price paid for a painting
Van Gogh	36			
Kahlo				
Picasso				

C Listen 🎧 Kevin and Lucy are now listening to an art museum tour. Complete the last two columns of the chart.

D Group work Discuss these questions.

- Do you like to visit art museums?
- What kind of art do you like?
- Have you taken photos of yourself? How did they look?

Activity 3 **Group work** Look at these pictures. Then discuss the questions below.

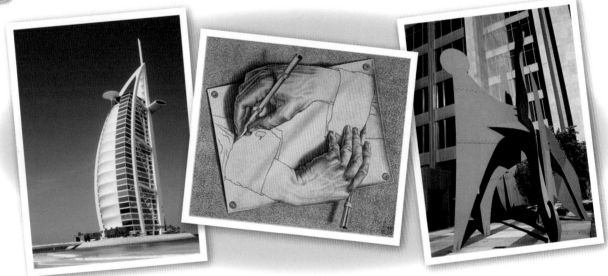

- What does each picture show? Which do you like the best?
- Do you have a favorite artist? Are there any artists you don't like?
- What pictures or posters do you have in your room? What do they say about you?

"The first picture is a building. It's shaped like a . . ."

Activity 4 **Communication task** Work in pairs. One of you should look at Task 16 on page 82, and the other at Task 36 on page 90. You're going to learn about two more artists.

Self-study For extra grammar, listening, and vocabulary practice, go to pages 120–121.

15A Remembering

Activity 1 **A** **Pair work** Describe these pictures of the same person's desk 15 years ago and today. Then discuss the questions below.

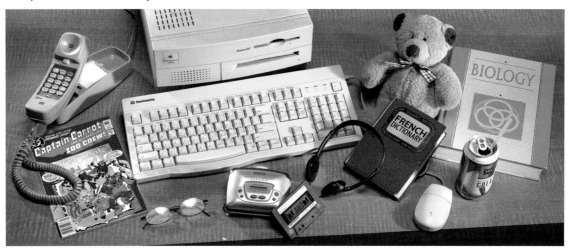

- Do you think the person is male or female? Why?
- What do you think the person was like 15 years ago?
- What do you think the person is like now?
- How do you think the person has changed in the last 15 years?

"I think the person is . . . because there's . . . on the desk."

"I'm not so sure. There's also . . ."

B **Join another pair** Discuss these questions.

- How have you changed since you were a child?
- How is your life better now than it was then? How is it worse?

"I never used to worry about anything. I'm more serious now."

"Actually, I'm less serious now. I . . ."

Activity 2 A **Pair work** Look at these pictures of Sarah, her son Bill, and her granddaughter Jenny. How do Sarah and Bill look different now?

Sarah in 1967

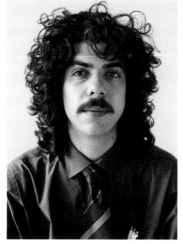
Bill in 1987

Sarah, Bill, and Jenny now

"Sarah has shorter hair now. And her hair looks straighter."

B **Listen** 🎧 Sarah and Bill are talking about their lives when they were 20 years old. Write *S* for Sarah and *B* for Bill.

At the age of 20, who . . . ?	
_S_ wore a flower in his / her hair	_____ played guitar in a band
_____ studied in Europe	_____ had a motorcycle accident
_____ had a big record collection	_____ loved sports
_____ dropped out of college	_____ learned to drive a car

C **Listen** 🎧 Sarah and Bill are now talking about their lives when they were 12 years old. Write *S* for Sarah and *B* for Bill.

At the age of 12, who . . . ?	
_____ had to share a room	_____ liked vegetables
_____ had a younger brother and an older sister	_____ enjoyed school
_____ had never been away from home	_____ liked vacations more than school
_____ sang songs all the time	_____ liked the same sports as Jenny

D **Group work** Discuss these questions.

- What did you like about being 12 years old? What did you dislike?
- Imagine you could be 12 for one day. What would you do?
- What was the best year of your life? Why?
- What's the best age to be? Why?
- What's your favorite childhood memory?

"I remember I liked school but disliked gym class. The teacher was . . ."

15B Historical places

Activity 1

A Pair work Where are these popular tourist sites? When were they built? Make guesses and match the items. Then go to page 93 to check your answers.

Mexico
Egypt

26th century BCE
2nd century BCE

Pyramid of the Sun, Teotihuacán

Great Pyramid of Giza

Korea
China

7th–10th century
14th–17th century

Great Wall

Gyeongju

Japan
Turkey

6th century
17th century

Kiyomizu Temple

Hagia Sophia

France
the U.S.

19th century
20th century

Rockefeller Center

Eiffel Tower

"Do you think the Pyramid of the Sun is older than the Great Pyramid?"

B Pair work Discuss these questions.

- What places would you most like to visit? Why?
- Can you think of other popular old tourist sites?

C Listen 🎧 You will hear tours of some of the places from part A. Complete the sentences.

1. Teotihuacán was the Aztec ___capital___ . It was dedicated to the _____ .
2. The Great Wall was built in the _____ Dynasty. Its purpose was to _____ .
3. *Kiyomizu* means "_____ ." People used to _____ from the veranda.
4. Rockefeller Center was built in the _____ . There's a great view from the _____ .

D Listen again 🎧 When is the best time to visit each place?

1. Teotihuacán: _____
2. The Great Wall: _____
3. Kiyomizu Temple: _____
4. Rockefeller Center: _____

Activity 2

Pair work List five important historical places in your country. Then discuss these questions.

- Which of these places have you visited?
- Who did you go with?
- What do you remember about it?
- What other places would you like to visit?

"I visited the statue of . . . . I went with my teacher and classmates."

"My family took me to see . . ."

Activity 3

A Pair work Can you match the events with the dates? Make guesses. Then go to page 93 to check your answers.

John Lennon was murdered on December 8, ___1980___ .	1969
Neil Armstrong first stepped on the moon on July 20, _____ .	1970
The first 747 jumbo jet flight was on January 21, _____ .	1980
A devastating tsunami struck the Indian Ocean on December 26, _____ .	1989
Princess Diana died on August 31, _____ .	1997
New York City's Twin Towers were destroyed on September 11, _____ .	2001
The Berlin Wall fell on November 9, _____ .	2004

B Pair work Which events in part A do you remember? How did you feel when they happened?

"I remember when the tsunami struck. I was . . ."

C Join another pair Discuss these questions.

- What was the most important event in your country's history?
- Who was the most important person in the history of your country?
- What was the most important world event during your lifetime?

"The most important event in my country's history was . . ."

Self-study For extra grammar, listening, and vocabulary practice, go to pages 122–123.

16A What's so funny?

A **Pair work** What is happening in each picture? Which situation is the funniest? Which is the least funny?

"In the first picture, the man is taking his foot out of a pan of yellow paint."

B **Pair work** Read about these actors. Then discuss the questions below.

Rowan Atkinson plays Mr. Bean, a silly Englishman who always gets into accidents. He never speaks, but he makes funny noises.

American actress Reese Witherspoon is known for both her dramatic and comedic roles. One of her most famous roles is that of Elle Woods in the movie comedy *Legally Blond*.

Hong Kong native Jackie Chan is an actor whose movies are popular around the world. He performs hilarious physical comedy and amazing stunts.

- Do you know any of these actors? Who do you think is the funniest?
- Who's the funniest comedian where you live?
- What's the most popular comedy show where you live? What's it like?
- What's the funniest movie you've ever seen? Why was it funny?

"I think Jackie Chan is the funniest. He always . . ."

Activity 2 **A** **Pair work** Look at these words. Write them in the correct columns.

| chuckle | giggle | hilarious | hysterical | physical comedy | slapstick |
| comical | guffaw | humorous | parody | satire | snicker |

Words for "funny"	Words for "laugh"	Types of humor
comical		

B **Pair work** Describe a comedian you like. Use words from part A and your own ideas.

"I think Jackie Chan is hysterical. His use of physical comedy is hilarious, and . . ."

Activity 3 **A** **Listen** You will hear the beginning of three funny stories. Can you guess the punch lines at the end? Check (✔) your guesses.

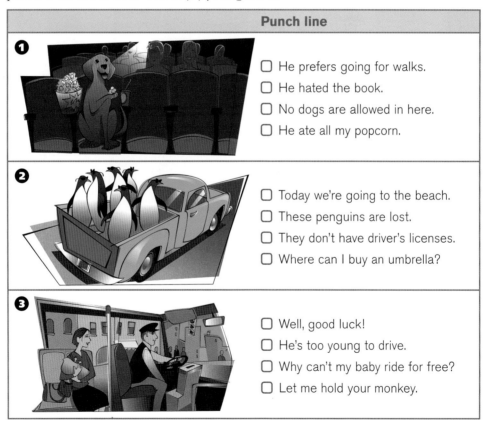

Punch line
❶ ▢ He prefers going for walks. ▢ He hated the book. ▢ No dogs are allowed in here. ▢ He ate all my popcorn.
❷ ▢ Today we're going to the beach. ▢ These penguins are lost. ▢ They don't have driver's licenses. ▢ Where can I buy an umbrella?
❸ ▢ Well, good luck! ▢ He's too young to drive. ▢ Why can't my baby ride for free? ▢ Let me hold your monkey.

B **Listen** Now listen to the complete stories. Did you guess correctly?

C **Listen again** Which story do you think was the funniest?

Activity 4 **Communication task** Work in groups of three. One of you should look at Task 17 on page 82, another at Task 40 on page 91, and another at Task 42 on page 92. You're going to tell some funny stories.

16B That's hilarious!

A **Work alone** Look at these cartoons. Rank each one from *1* (the funniest) to *5* (the least funny).

"What a vacation—we swam with dolphins!"

FASHION MAGAZINE

IN   OUT   BACK IN AGAIN

B **Pair work** Compare your answers. Do you find the same things funny?

"Why do you find that one funny? I chose it as the least funny."

C **Join another pair** Discuss these questions.

- How often do you look at the comics in the newspaper? Do you have a favorite?
- How often do you watch cartoons on TV? Do you have a favorite?
- Do you and your family laugh at the same things? How about you and your friends?

"I always look at the comics. My favorite is . . ."

Activity 2 **A Listen** Look at the pictures. You will hear the beginning of two stories. When you hear a "beep," guess how each story ends.

1

2

B Listen again You will now hear the rest of the stories. Did you guess correctly?

C Pair work Discuss these questions.

- Which story was funnier? Why?
- Have you heard any similar stories? What happened?

Activity 3 **A Pair work** Read these jokes. Which do you think is the funniest?

Q: Why does our teacher wear sunglasses?
A: Because the class is so bright.

Q: Why is the letter T like an island?
A: Because it's in the middle of water.

Q: Why was the baby ant confused?
A: Because all her uncles were ants.

Q: What building has the most stories?
A: The library.

B Communication task Work in groups of three. One of you should look at Task 18 on page 83, another at Task 38 on page 90, and another at Task 43 on page 92. You're going to tell some jokes.

Self-study For extra grammar, listening, and vocabulary practice, go to pages 124–125.

Units 13–16 Expansion

How to play

1 Work in groups.
Each player places
a token such as
a paper clip,
a pen cap, or
an eraser
on **Start**.

2 Take turns. Roll a
die, move that
number of spaces,
and say at least
one sentence about
the topic.

3 Other players
can ask follow-up
questions.

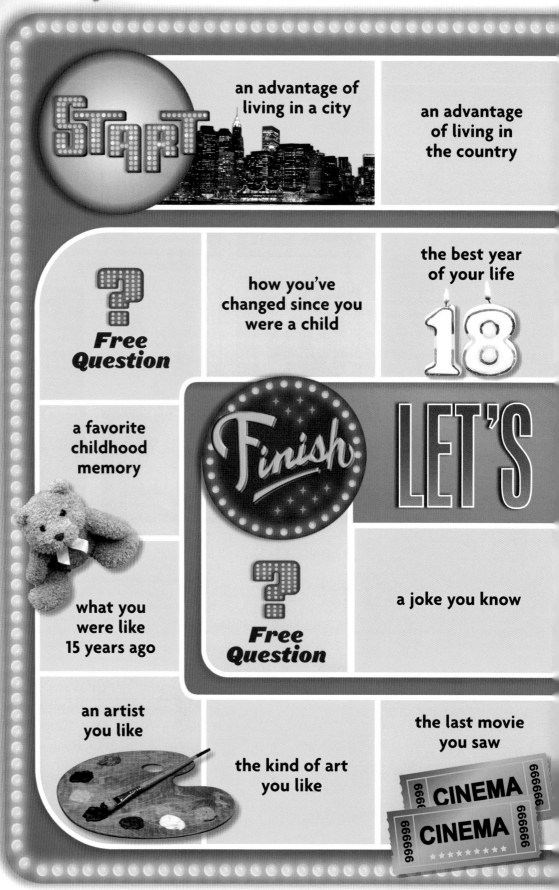

Start

an advantage of living in a city

an advantage of living in the country

? Free Question

how you've changed since you were a child

the best year of your life

a favorite childhood memory

Finish

LET'S

what you were like 15 years ago

? Free Question

a joke you know

an artist you like

the kind of art you like

the last movie you saw

CINEMA

CINEMA

what you like about where you live

? **Free Question**

a city you'd like to visit

things people should do to stay safe

an important historical event in your lifetime

a historical place you've visited

the funniest person you know

a recent crime you've heard about

TALK ABOUT...

the funniest movie you've ever seen

something you enjoy doing with your family

something funny that happened to you

a cartoon character you like

your favorite comedy show

your taste in music

? **Free Question**

a song you love

a band you like

your favorite singer

Communication tasks

Task 1
(page 3)

A How can you improve these things? Ask questions and complete the chart.

Speaking	Listening	Vocabulary
Ask a lot of questions. Speak English with your friends outside of class. Say new phrases aloud so you can practice them easily.	Watch movies in English.	

"How can I improve my listening?"   *"You can watch movies in English."*

B Do you have any other ideas? Add them to the chart. Then share them with the class.

Task 2
(page 5)

A Ask your partner these questions, and check (✔) the answers. Then answer your partner's questions.

1. How fast do you usually walk?
   ☐ fast   ☐ average speed   ☐ slowly

2. What do you prefer to wear?
   ☐ the latest fashions   ☐ clothes that are always in style   ☐ whatever's comfortable

3. What do you prefer to do in your free time?
   ☐ read a book   ☐ watch TV at home   ☐ go dancing with friends

4. What kind of social event do you prefer?
   ☐ a crowded party   ☐ a small gathering   ☐ a dinner with one person

5. When do you arrive for appointments?
   ☐ early   ☐ on time   ☐ late

6. How does your bedroom look?
   ☐ very neat   ☐ a little messy   ☐ very messy

B Now use these words to describe your partner's personality.

active	laid-back	neat	organized	relaxed
disorganized	messy	nervous	outgoing	shy

"I think you're laid-back but a little disorganized. Am I right?"

"I agree I'm laid-back, but I'm really very organized."

Task 3
(page 7)

A Walk around the class. Find one person who answers "yes" to each question. Then ask a follow-up question. Write the information in the chart.

Who . . . ?	Name	Extra information
has a part-time job		
has a younger brother		
plays a musical instrument		
collects something unusual		

"Do you have a part-time job?"

"Yes, I do."

"Really? Where do you work?"

B Go back to your group, and tell them what you learned.

Task 4
(page 11)

A Sit back-to-back. Imagine it's 2:00 p.m. and you're on a train. Your partner is Terry's roommate. Call your partner and leave this message for Terry.

• My train is late.
• I'll meet Terry at Central Café at 4:00.
• I'll call if there are more delays.
• Terry can call me on my cell phone at 343-555-0715.

B It's now 3:00 p.m. You're still on the train, and it's even later than expected. Your cell phone rings. Answer the phone.

Task 5
(page 13)

A Look at this recipe with your partner. Try to remember the main points.

French crepes

Ingredients
■ 100 grams of flour
■ 30 grams of sugar
■ 2 eggs
■ 300 milliliters of milk
■ 30 grams of butter
■ lemon juice
■ honey

Instructions
1. First, mix the flour, sugar, and eggs together.
2. Then add the milk little by little. Keep stirring.
3. Next, melt and add the butter. Mix together and wait for 30 minutes.
4. After that, heat a little butter in a pan.
5. Pour a little mixture into the pan, and fry on each side.
6. Serve with a little lemon juice and honey or sugar.

B Join the other pair. Find out how to make Swiss muesli. Then explain how to make French crepes.

"First, you need 100 grams of flour, 30 grams of sugar, 2 eggs, and . . ."

Task 6

(page 17)

Imagine you are in London, England. It's 10:00 a.m. Call your friend in Sydney, Australia. Ask each other about the weather.

Yesterday morning
warm and sunny

Yesterday afternoon
hot with strong winds

Last night
warm and wet

Earlier this morning
cool and clear

Right now
warmer but cloudy

- What time is it in Sydney now?
- What's the weather like there?
- What was the weather like yesterday?

Task 7

(page 25)

Ask five Yes / No questions to guess one another's jobs. Use these jobs or your own ideas.

comedian   house painter   dentist   no job: still a student

- Do you make a lot of money?
- Do you need special training?
- Do you entertain people?
- Are you a . . . ?

Task 8

(page 27)

A Ask your partner about these activities. Write the answers below.

Have you been to any amusement parks?

_____

If so, what did you like about them?

_____

If not, would you like to visit one? Why or why not?

_____

Have you tried snowboarding?

_____

If so, what was it like?

_____

If not, would you like to try it? Why or why not?

_____

B Compare your answers with another pair. Then discuss these questions.

- Which of the four activities do you each prefer?
- Which activity is the least popular? Why do you think so?

Task 9

(page 33)

Read and explain these instructions to your group. Then choose a game to play.

"I went on a trip . . . "
The first player starts a list of things. The next player remembers the list and adds one more thing.

Example:
A: I went on a trip and took an umbrella.
B: I went on a trip and took an umbrella and a guidebook.
C: I went on a trip and took an umbrella, a guidebook, and my sister.

The first player who makes a mistake starts a new list.

Task 10

(page 35)

A Your partner will ask you questions. Guess the answers.

B Now ask your partner these questions, and check (✓) the answers. Then tell your partner the answers.

1. What were the first wheels made of?
   ☐ stone   ☐ wood   ☐ metal

2. Who were the first travelers in a hot-air balloon?
   ☐ American scientists   ☐ French inventors   ☐ farm animals

3. Where can you ride the world's fastest train?
   ☐ France   ☐ Japan   ☐ China

4. Which city had the world's first subway system?
   ☐ Paris   ☐ Tokyo   ☐ London

5. How many new bicycles are sold each year?
   ☐ 10 million   ☐ 100 million   ☐ 1 billion

6. In which countries must you drive on the left?
   ☐ Australia   ☐ Japan   ☐ India   ☐ Indonesia   ☐ Malaysia   ☐ Thailand

Answers: 1. stone   2. farm animals   3. China   4. London   5. 100 million   6. All of them

Task 11

(page 41)

A Look at these pictures from Tom and Kelly's vacation. Decide what happened after each picture was taken. Then describe the vacation.

"Tom and Kelly went fishing one day. Tom was trying to bring in a fish when . . ."

B Listen to your partner's description of Paul and Diane's vacation. What did the two vacations have in common?

Task 12

(page 47)

A Look at these ice-cream machines. Ask and answer questions to complete the chart.

	EZ Ice Cream	Play and Freeze
What it is	a gadget that makes ice cream in four hours	
How it works	automatically stirs the ice-cream mixture to create ice cream in your freezer	
Special features	battery-operated, recipes included	
Price	$39.99	

"What does the Play and Freeze do?"

B Which machine do you think is a better value?

Task 13

(page 48)

A Look at the advantages of having a bird or cat as a pet. Then look at the disadvantages of having a dog or goldfish. Add one more example to each.

"Another advantage of having a bird as a pet is . . ."

	Advantages	**Disadvantages**
	They're inexpensive to feed. Some can "talk." _____	_____ _____
	_____ _____ _____	They need a lot of attention. Some are expensive to feed. _____
	They're usually quiet. They can be fun to play with. _____	_____ _____ _____
	_____ _____ _____	They can be kind of boring. The bowl often needs cleaning. _____

B Join the other pair, and share your information. Which animal makes the best pet?

Task 14

(page 55)

A Read this story. Try to remember the main points.

Teen Pays Fine With Pennies

A teenager in the United States recently received a $100 ticket for jaywalking. He paid the fine, but he didn't pay by check or credit card. Darren Olson went to court to pay his ticket with bags and bags of pennies. He had over 10,000 pennies in the bags. A court representative took the money with her to the bank while the teen waited. The bank counted the money and gave her $100 in bills. "I actually got a few pennies back," Olson laughed.

B Look at these headlines and pictures for your partners' stories. Then ask and answer questions about the stories. Take turns.

Swan Falls In Love With Boat

Emu Chases Girl Up Tree

- Where did the story take place?
- What happened (in the end)?
- Why do you think . . . ?

Task 15

(page 59)

A Read this information about Shanghai. Then answer your partner's questions.

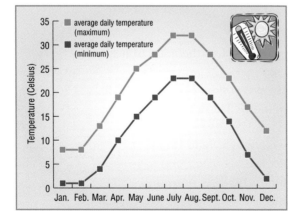

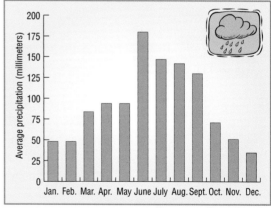

Source: www.bbc.co.uk/weather

Must see: The Bund – interesting old buildings along the river
Must do: Go up Oriental Pearl Tower – a great view of the city
Visit the Shanghai Museum – wonderful old Chinese works of art
Must eat: Shanghai dumplings – meat dumplings that are fried and then steamed

B Now ask your partner questions about Rio de Janeiro. Find out about the weather. Then ask for recommendations on what to see, do, and eat.

Task 16

(page 65)

Ask questions to find out about Andy Warhol. Then discuss the questions below.

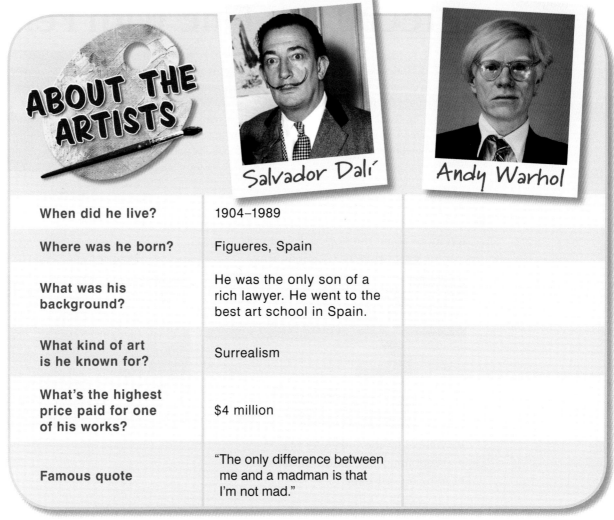

ABOUT THE ARTISTS

Salvador Dalí

Andy Warhol

	Salvador Dalí	Andy Warhol
When did he live?	1904–1989	
Where was he born?	Figueres, Spain	
What was his background?	He was the only son of a rich lawyer. He went to the best art school in Spain.	
What kind of art is he known for?	Surrealism	
What's the highest price paid for one of his works?	$4 million	
Famous quote	"The only difference between me and a madman is that I'm not mad."	

- What information about Dalí and Warhol surprised you?
- What do the quotes tell you about them?

Task 17

(page 71)

Read this story and tell it to your partners. Use the notes to help you.

Every morning, Mrs. Brown wakes up her son Tim.

But one morning, Tim said, "I don't want to go to school today."

"Give me two good reasons why you don't want to go," she said.

"All right," he said. "One, the kids hate me. And two, the teachers hate me."

"Don't be silly. Hurry up and get ready for school," she said.

"Give me two good reasons why I have to go to school," he said.

"All right," she said. "One, you're 52 years old. And two, you're the principal!"

Notes:

Every morning –
Mrs. Brown – wakes up – son Tim
Tim: Don't want to go to school
Mom: Two reasons why
Tim: 1) kids hate me
    2) teachers hate me
Mom: Hurry up, get ready
Tim: Two reasons why
Mom: 1) 52
    2) principal

Task 18
(page 73)

Read each joke to your partners. Wait for them to guess the answer. Then tell them the answer.

Q: What does a white hat become if you drop in into the Red Sea?

A: Wet.

Q: Why do birds fly south for the winter?

A: Because it's too far to walk.

Q: What two things can't you have for breakfast?

A: Lunch and dinner.

Task 19
(page 3)

A How can you improve these things? Ask questions and complete the chart.

Speaking	Listening	Vocabulary
	Watch movies in English. Don't translate what you hear into your native language.	Highlight new words in this book.

"How can I improve my vocabulary?"   "You can highlight new words in this book."

B Do you have any other ideas? Add them to the chart. Then share them with the class.

Task 20
(page 7)

A Walk around the class. Find one person who answers "yes" to each question. Then ask a follow-up question. Write the information in the chart.

Who . . . ?	Name	Extra information
loves to cook		
has an older sister		
belongs to a club		
can say "Thank you" in four languages		

"Do you love to cook?"

"Yes, I do."

"Really? What's your favorite dish to make?"

B Go back to your group, and tell them what you learned.

Task 21

(page 3)

A How can you improve these things? Ask questions and complete the chart.

Speaking	Listening	Vocabulary
Ask a lot of questions.		Highlight new words in this book. Use words you just learned when you talk. Write new words in a vocabulary notebook.

"How can I improve my speaking?"   *"You can ask a lot of questions."*

B Do you have any other ideas? Add them to the chart. Then share them with the class.

Task 22

(page 5)

A Answer your partner's questions. Then ask your partner these questions, and check (✓) the answers.

1. How often do you talk on the phone?
   ☐ all the time   ☐ often   ☐ not much

2. What do you do when you shop?
   ☐ list things to buy   ☐ mostly buy things you need   ☐ buy whatever looks good

3. What do you prefer to do in your free time?
   ☐ watch TV or read   ☐ play sports   ☐ sleep

4. When do you do your homework?
   ☐ as soon as you get home ☐ after you relax for a while ☐ at the last minute

5. Where do you write notes in class?
   ☐ on the textbook pages   ☐ in a separate notebook   ☐ nowhere

6. What do you think when waiting for a train or bus?
   ☐ It's going to be on time.   ☐ It might be a little late.   ☐ It's going to be very late.

B Now use these words to describe your partner's personality.

active	laid-back	neat	outgoing	relaxed
disorganized	messy	nervous	organized	shy

"I think you're laid-back but a little disorganized. Am I right?"

"I agree I'm laid-back, but I'm really very organized."

Task 23

(page 7)

A Walk around the class. Find one person who answers "yes" to each question. Then ask a follow-up question. Write the information in the chart.

Who . . . ?	Name	Extra information
has a pet		
lives in an apartment		
wants to go to graduate school		
can say "Hello" in four languages		

"Do you have a pet?"

"Yes, I do. I have a cat."

"Really? What's its name?"

B Go back to your group, and tell them what you learned.

Task 24

(page 11)

A Sit back-to-back. Imagine it's 2:00 p.m. and you're at home. Your roommate, Terry, is out. Your partner calls and wants to leave a message for Terry. Take the message.

B It's now 3:00 p.m. Call your partner and give this information.

- Terry is still out.
- Terry's cell phone is at home.
- Terry is probably at the café.
- The phone number of the café is 767-555-1625.

Task 25

(page 13)

A Look at this recipe with your partner. Try to remember the main points.

Swiss muesli

Ingredients

- 50 grams of nuts
- 1 apple
- 250 grams of oatmeal
- 30 milliliters of honey
- juice of 1/2 lemon
- 250 milliliters of yogurt or milk
- fruit

Instructions

1. First, chop the nuts and grate the apple.
2. Next, add the nuts and apple to the oatmeal, honey, and lemon juice.
3. After that, add the milk or yogurt. Mix together well.
4. Put in the refrigerator for 30 minutes.
5. Remove from the refrigerator. Then put fruit on top.
6. Serve for breakfast or as a dessert.

B Join the other pair. Explain how to make Swiss muesli. Then find out how to make French crepes.

"First, you need 50 grams of nuts, 1 apple, 250 grams of oatmeal, and . . ."

Task 26

(page 17)

Imagine you are in Sydney, Australia. It's 7:00 p.m. Your friend calls you from London, England. Ask each other about the weather.

Yesterday morning
hot and very sunny

Yesterday afternoon
very rainy

Last night
cool with light rain

Earlier today
warm and windy

Right now
still warm

- What time is it in London now?
- What's the weather like there?
- What was the weather like yesterday?

Task 27

(page 25)

Ask five Yes / No questions to guess one another's jobs. Use these jobs or your own ideas.

dancer   bus driver   interpreter   no job: unemployed

- Do you make a lot of money?
- Do you need special training?
- Do you entertain people?
- Are you a . . . ?

Task 28

(page 27)

A Ask your partner about these activities. Write the answers below.

Have you been to any museums?

_____

If so, what did you like about them?

_____

If not, would you like to visit one? Why or why not?

_____

Have you played miniature golf?

_____

If so, what was it like?

_____

If not, would you like to try it? Why or why not?

_____

B Compare your answers with another pair. Then discuss these questions.

- Which of the four activities do you each prefer?
- Which activity is the least popular? Why do you think so?

Task 29

(page 33)

Read and explain these instructions to your group. Then choose a game to play.

"Who am I?"

The first player leaves the room. The other players choose a famous person. The first player returns and asks "Who am I?" Each player gives three clues.

> *Example:*
> **A:** You're a movie star.
> **B:** You're very good-looking.
> **A:** You have blond hair.

The first player has only three chances to guess the famous person.

Task 30

(page 35)

A Your partner will ask you questions. Guess the answers.

B Now ask your partner these questions, and check (✓) the answers. Then tell your partner the answers.

1. Where can you travel on the world's longest subway system?
   ☐ Seoul   ☐ New York City   ☐ London

2. How long was the first plane flight across the Atlantic Ocean?
   ☐ 23 hours   ☐ 33 hours   ☐ 43 hours

3. Which country has the most cars per person?
   ☐ the U.S.   ☐ Canada   ☐ Australia

4. Which country had the first public bus system?
   ☐ France   ☐ Mexico   ☐ India

5. How many new cars are sold each year?
   ☐ 4.2 million   ☐ 42 million   ☐ 420 million

6. In which countries must you drive on the right?
   ☐ Brazil ☐ Canada ☐ China ☐ Korea ☐ Russia ☐ Singapore

Answers: 1. London   2. 33 hours   3. Australia   4. France   5. 4.2 million   6. All of them except Singapore

Task 31

(page 41)

A Look at these pictures from Paul and Diane's vacation. Decide what happened after each picture was taken. Then describe the vacation.

"Paul and Diane went scuba diving one day. Paul was going to get in the water when . . ."

B Listen to your partner's description of Tom and Kelly's vacation. What did the two vacations have in common?

Task 32

(page 47)

A Look at these ice-cream machines. Ask and answer questions to complete the chart.

	EZ Ice Cream	Play and Freeze
What it is		a ball that makes ice cream in only twenty minutes
How it works		shaking and rolling the ball causes ice in the outer part to freeze the ice-cream mixture in the inner part
Special features		no batteries required, recipes included
Price		$29.99

"What does the EZ Ice Cream do?"

B Which machine do you think is a better value?

Task 33

(page 48)

A Look at the disadvantages of having a bird or cat as a pet. Then look at the advantages of having a dog or goldfish. Add one more example to each.

"Another disadvantage of having a bird as a pet is . . ."

	Advantages	Disadvantages
	_____ _____ _____	It's cruel to keep them in a cage. They can be noisy. _____
	They make loyal friends. They act as protection. _____	_____ _____ _____
	_____ _____ _____	They may ignore you. They're sometimes moody. _____
	They're calming to look at. They don't need a lot of attention. _____	_____ _____ _____

B Join the other pair, and share your information. Which animal makes the best pet?

Task 34

(page 55)

A Read this story. Try to remember the main points.

Swan Falls In Love With Boat

A confused swan in central Japan has fallen in love with a swan-shaped boat. The swan is not allowing anyone to take the boat onto the lake. Boat owner Hideo Nakayama is not amused. "At first I thought it was funny, but now I'm losing business," he claimed, though many people have come to see the love-struck swan. The owner hopes the swan will find a real mate soon, but he is worried because swans mate for life.

B Look at these headlines and pictures for your partners' stories. Then ask and answer questions about the stories. Take turns.

Emu Chases Girl Up Tree

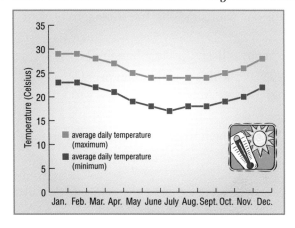

Teen Pays Fine With Pennies

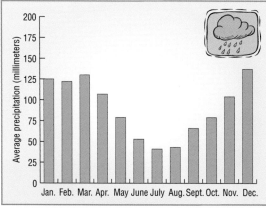

- Where did the story take place?
- What happened (in the end)?
- Why do you think . . . ?

Task 35

(page 59)

A Ask your partner questions about Shanghai. Find out about the weather. Then ask for recommendations on what to see, do, and eat.

B Read this information about Rio de Janeiro. Answer your partner's questions.

Source: www.bbc.co.uk/weather

Must see: Copacabana Beach – beautiful beach near hotels and restaurants

Must do: Visit the Native American Museum – old tools, jewelry, and clothes
Go up Sugar Loaf Mountain – fantastic views of the city

Must eat: Feijoada – a stew made with meat and black beans

Ask questions to find out about Salvador Dalí. Then discuss the questions below.

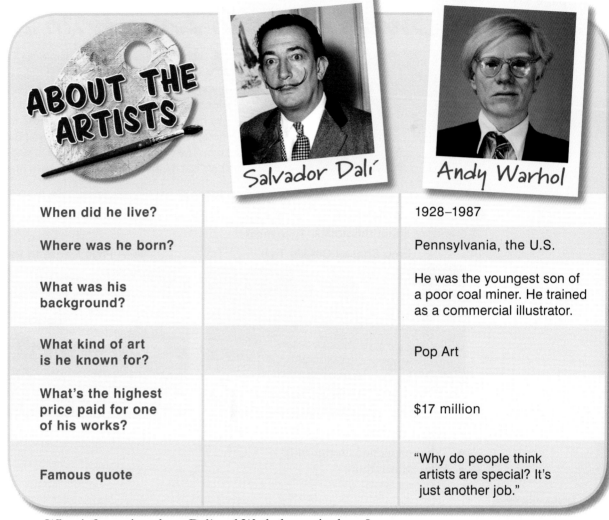

	Salvador Dalí	Andy Warhol
When did he live?		1928–1987
Where was he born?		Pennsylvania, the U.S.
What was his background?		He was the youngest son of a poor coal miner. He trained as a commercial illustrator.
What kind of art is he known for?		Pop Art
What's the highest price paid for one of his works?		$17 million
Famous quote		"Why do people think artists are special? It's just another job."

- What information about Dalí and Warhol surprised you?
- What do the quotes tell you about them?

Ask five Yes / No questions to guess one another's jobs. Use these jobs or your own ideas.

   fashion model   farmer   army officer   no job: retired

- Do you make a lot of money?
- Do you need special training?
- Do you entertain people?
- Are you a . . . ?

Read each joke to your partners. Wait for them to guess the answer. Then tell them the answer.

Q: Who never gets his hair wet in the shower?

A: A bald man.

Q: Where does success come before work?

A: In a dictionary.

Q: What does a dog become after it's six years old?

A: Seven years old.

A Read this story. Try to remember the main points.

Emu Chases Girl Up Tree

Australian firefighters rescued a girl after an angry emu chased her up a tree. Lindsay Carlyle, 10, saw the emu in her backyard and tried to pet the bird. The emu chased her, and Lindsay escaped to the nearest tree. She climbed high into the tree, beyond the reach of the flightless bird. The emu stayed near the tree until firefighters arrived. "Lindsay is fine now," said her mother. Firefighters moved the bird safely to the wild.

B Look at these headlines and pictures for your partners' stories. Then ask and answer questions about the stories. Take turns.

Teen Pays Fine With Pennies

Swan Falls In Love With Boat

- Where did the story take place?
- What happened (in the end)?
- Why do you think . . . ?

Read this story and tell it to your partners. Use the notes to help you.

One day, two students went to the beach and missed an important exam.

The next day, they said to their teacher, "Our car got a flat tire on the way to school, so we missed the exam. Can we take it tomorrow?"

"OK," she said.

So they studied all night for the exam. The next day, when they arrived, the teacher said, "One of you go to Classroom A, and the other to Classroom B."

They sat down and looked at the exam paper. There were only four words on the paper: "Which tire was it?"

Notes:
One day – two students –
beach – missed exam
Students: Flat tire –
missed exam – tomorrow?
Teacher: OK
Studied all night
Next day
Teacher: One, Room A
Other, Room B
Exam paper – four words:
"Which tire was it?"

Task 41

(page 33)

Read and explain these instructions to your group. Then choose a game to play.

Spelling Bee
Everyone writes three challenging English words. The first player asks the second player to spell a word. If the second player spells it correctly, he or she gets a point. If it's incorrect, the third player tries to spell the word and get the point.

Example:
A: How do you spell "accommodation"?
B: It's spelled A-C-C-O-M-O-D-A-T-I-O-N.
A: Sorry, that's not correct. How do you spell "accommodation"?
C: A-C-C-O-M-M-O-D-A-T-I-O-N.
A: Correct! You get one point.

The player with the most points wins the game.

Task 42

(page 71)

Read this story and tell it to your partners. Use the notes to help you.

One day, Professor Jones gave a 100-point test to his class. At the end of the lesson, the professor collected the tests. He took them back to his office to grade. One student, Billy, had attached a $100 bill and a note to his test. The note read, "One dollar for every point."

The next day, the professor handed back the tests. He also gave Billy an envelope. When Billy looked in the envelope, he found $90 and a note. The note read, "Here is your change."

Notes:
One day – Professor Jones – 100-point test
End of lesson –
    collected tests – office
Billy's test: $100 bill attached + note: "$1 for every point"
Next day – tests back
Envelope for Billy – $90 + note: "Here's your change"

Task 43

(page 73)

Read each joke to your partners. Wait for them to guess the answer. Then tell them the answer.

Q: Which is the best hand to write with?

A: Neither. Use a pen instead.

Q: If you have four oranges in one hand and five oranges in the other, what do you have?

A: Big hands.

Q: How many months have 28 days?

A: They all do.

92 *Communication tasks*

Answers

Lesson 7A
(page 31)

Here are the scores and the analysis for the quiz from Activity 2B.

21 or more	Unbelievable! Are you planning to become a professional athlete?
15–20	You're very active in sports. Do you have time for anything else?
10–14	You're involved in sports, but you have time for other interests, too.
4–9	You take an interest in sports, but maybe you watch more than you play?
3 or less	So sports aren't your thing. That's OK – not everyone likes sports.

Lesson 8A
(page 35)

The meanings of the signs from Activity 3A are:

1. Bike lane   2. Pay to enter downtown   3. Parking lot   4. Buses only   5. No cars

Lesson 9B
(page 42)

All the pictures show Australia.

Lesson 11B
(page 50)

Here are the scores and the analysis for the quiz from Activity 2A.

36–48	You're so concerned about the environment, it's unbelievable! Are there even more things you do to protect the environment?
24–35	You're very environmentally aware. You care about and respect the world around you.
12–23	You do some things to protect the environment, but there's always room for improvement.
0–11	You're not concerned about the environment at all. Be aware of the things you can do. Everything you do will help.

Lesson 15B
(page 68)

The correct answers for Activity 1A are:

Pyramid of the Sun, Teotihuacán	Mexico	2nd century BCE
Great Pyramid of Giza	Egypt	26th century BCE
Great Wall	China	14th–17th century
Gyeongju	Korea	7th–10th century
Kiyomizu Temple	Japan	17th century
Hagia Sophia	Turkey	6th century
Rockefeller Center	the U. S.	20th century
Eiffel Tower	France	19th century

Lesson 15B
(page 69)

The correct answers for Activity 3A are:

John Lennon was murdered on December 8, 1980.
Neil Armstrong first stepped on the moon on July 20, 1969.
The first 747 jumbo jet flight was on January 21, 1970.
A devastating tsunami struck the Indian Ocean on December 26, 2004.
Princess Diana died on August 31, 1997.
New York City's Twin Towers were destroyed on September 11, 2001.
The Berlin Wall fell on November 9, 1989.

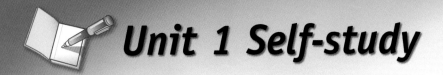

Unit 1 Self-study

A 🎧 Listen and practice.

Present, past, and future: Review		

Present	What**'s** your name?
	   My name **is** Elizabeth.
		Is your nickname Beth?
		   No, it **isn't**. It**'s** Lizzie.

	What **do** you **do**?
	   I**'m** a teacher.
		Do you **teach** English?
		   No, I **don't**. I **teach** Spanish.

Past	Where **were** you born?
	   I **was** born in Lima, Peru.
		Did you **grow up** there?
		   Yes, I **did**. I **lived** there until I **was** 18.

	When **did** you **move** here?
	   I **moved** here in 2005.
		Did your family **come**, too?
		   Yes, they **did**. We all **came**.

Future	Where **will** you **be** next year?
	   I**'ll be** in school. I**'ll be** a student.
		Will you **be** here tomorrow?
		   No, I **won't**. I**'ll be** at work.

B Complete the conversation. Use the correct form of the verbs in parentheses.

A: Excuse me. ___Is___ (be) the coffee good here?

B: Yes, it _____ (be). Wait. I know you. You _____ (be) in my English class
    this year. And I think you _____ (be) in my class last year. _____ you
    _____ (remember) me?

A: Sure! You _____ (sit) next to me last year. Our teacher _____ (be) Ms. Torres.

B: That _____ (be) right! So, _____ you _____ (have) a nice summer?

A: Yes, it _____ (be) fantastic! I _____ (spend) a month at the beach. What about you?

B: I _____ (work) at my uncle's café and _____ (make) a lot of money.

A: That's great. So, _____ you _____ (think) the teacher _____ (give) a lot of
    homework this weekend? She _____ (not give) us any last weekend.

B: I hope we _____ (not have) homework. I _____ (have) exciting plans.

A: Really? Not me. Next weekend, I _____ (stay) home and clean my apartment.

B: Well, it _____ (be) nice talking to you. I _____ (see) you tomorrow. Bye!

C Unscramble the questions. Then answer them.

1. name / what / your / is
   Q: _What is your name_____?   A: _____.

2. where / born / you / were
   Q: _____?   A: _____.

3. will / be / next / where / you / year
   Q: _____?   A: _____.

Self-study answer key

Unit 1

Grammar

B Is / is / 're / were / Do / remember / sat / was / 's / did / have / was / spent / worked / made / do / think / will give / didn't give / won't have / have / 'll stay / was / 'll see

C *Questions*
1. What is your name?
2. Where were you born?
3. Where will you be next year?

Possible answers
1. My name is (Yoshi).
2. I was born in (Osaka).
3. I'll be (in Tokyo) next year.

Listening
bag / China / spring / best / April / Palace / Wall / killed / left / looked / taxi

Vocabulary
1. solitary
2. peaceful
3. calm
4. icebreaker
5. talkative
6. appointment
7. outgoing
8. messy
9. laid-back
10. crowded
11. serious

```
I C E B R E A K E R C A
E A T O U T G O I N G C
S P L E V B B N O L N
M O K R S O C I A B L E
E S I A A N S E R I O U S
S N T E S O L I T A R Y
Y T I E E R V C E L U A
L M V O N C T R U B E Y
T E E V P E A C E F U L
N N E L A I D B A C K Z
R U N J C R O W D E D E
```

Unit 2

Grammar

B
1. Answering your phone in an elevator is rude.
2. It's friendly to touch someone on the arm when you're talking.
3. Making a phone call on the street is OK.
4. Calling someone late at night isn't polite.
5. It's rude to look at someone directly.
6. It's normal to offer a visitor something to eat and drink.
7. Shaking hands when you meet someone for the first time is common.
8. Changing first impressions is difficult.

C *Answers will vary.*

Listening
evening / eleven / noon / 555-1295 / meeting / dinner / eight / hotel / voice / 555-7729 / tomorrow

Vocabulary
Across
1. behavior
2. on hold
3. stand up
4. eye contact
5. cell phone
6. shake hands
7. exchange
8. message
9. rude
10. facial
11. psychologist
12. text message
Down
13. body language

Unit 3

Grammar

B *Answers will vary.*

C How much / how many / a few / much / a little / lamb / vegetables / many / potatoes / a cake / any / a little

Listening
300 / 4 / 1 / 250 / 25 / 1 / 160 / whites / almonds / 45 / heat / cool

Vocabulary
Across
1. spoonful
3. seafood
6. snack
8. recipe
9. bake
10. vegetables
11. appetizer
Down
2. flour
4. dessert
5. barbecue
6. spicy
7. breakfast

Unit 4

Grammar

B
1. If it's warm and sunny, I always walk to work.
2. I want to go to the beach if the weather is nice this weekend.
3. If it's cold outside, I sometimes feel depressed and lazy.
4. I want to have a picnic in the park if it isn't rainy tomorrow.
5. If you're indoors during a thunderstorm, disconnect the TV.
6. Protect yourself against frostbite if you're outdoors during a blizzard.
7. Don't go out in a boat if you're outdoors during a thunderstorm.
8. If you're outside in direct sunlight, use sunscreen.

C *Answers will vary.*

Listening
cloudy / 30 / rained / showers / Wednesday / thunderstorm / flooded / sunny / pictures / snowed / spring

Vocabulary
1. fall
2. irritable
3. cloudy
4. depressed
5. blizzard
6. typhoon
7. drought
8. thunderstorm
9. outdoors
10. forecast

Unit 5

Grammar

B
1. pleased / exciting / interesting / boring / bored
2. fascinating / fascinated / interesting / interested
3. surprising / amazing / interesting / thrilled

C *Answers will vary.*

Listening

dull / new / supportive / forward / late / overtime / money / boring / customers / busy / impatient

Vocabulary

1. lifeguard
2. retired
3. unemployed
4. interpreter
5. lunch break
6. workplace
7. promotion
8. professional
9. salary
10. pilot
11. hospital
12. supportive

```
P R O F E S S I O N A L
A W O R K P L A C E S C
N I L E L E R S A L A R Y C
T S U P P O R T I V E C
T R T E J M J U R L L
E A E S L O N Y E U R
R Y T P I T O E I C E
P R C I F I S M B I C B
R T V L E O P T R H B L
E J N O G N I L A E B L
T N N T U V T O Y D R L
E A A R A E A Y E V E A
R B N B R T U E V E A L
O J L O D Y N D J C K T
```

Unit 6

Grammar

B 1. a. didn't have to / would go, might go, *or* could go
   b. had / would go, might go, *or* could go
2. a. would make, might make, *or* could make / had
   b. didn't have to / would clean, might clean, *or* could clean
3. a. had / would cook, might cook, *or* could cook
   b. would rent, might rent, *or* could rent / didn't have

C 1. a   2. a   3. b

D *Answers will vary.*

Listening

shopping / DVDs / food / cook / band / Guitar / Friday / First / exciting / satisfying / famous

Vocabulary

Across
1. activity
2. creative
3. stimulating
4. inexpensive
5. educational
6. productively
7. rewarding
8. satisfying
9. laundry
10. museum
11. relaxing
12. feeding
13. fixing
Down
14. time-consuming

Unit 7

Grammar

B 1. volleyball
2. aerobics
3. sailing
4. yoga
5. hiking
6. table tennis
7. swimming
8. puzzle
9. weight training
10. Frisbee
11. skiing
12. Scrabble

C *Answers will vary.*

Listening

fan / soccer / goals / wider / basketball / high / teams / Olympics / Swimming / athletes / talent

Vocabulary

Across
1. checkers
6. athlete
8. team
10. watching
11. skill
Down
2. card
3. equipment
4. outdoor
5. volleyball
7. seasonal
9. luck

Unit 8

Grammar

B 1. the best / faster than / easier
2. the easiest / better than / the slowest / the worst
3. the most beautiful / the largest / the most crowded

C *Questions*
1. What's the worst transportation problem?
2. What's the best way to get to school?
3. Is it easier to get around by car or on foot?
4. What's the most beautiful city?
5. Is it cheaper to travel by subway or bus?
6. When is the most crowded time to travel?

Answers will vary.

Listening

lands / afternoon / rush / two / public / bus / 40 / taxi / express / highway / midnight

Vocabulary

1. driver
2. dangerous
3. subway
4. pedestrian
5. traffic jam
6. parking lot
7. comfort
8. memorable
9. motorbike
10. ridden
11. downtown
12. solution
13. directions

Unit 9

Grammar

B 1. Have / taken / spent / had
2. Did / go / went / Have / been / 've been
3. 've / taken / 've / taken / went / 've / been / 've heard
4. Did / enjoy / loved / 've been / was / liked / preferred

C *Answers will vary.*

Listening

two / dream / planning / wet / coast / cliffs / beach / second / Canyon / weather / souvenir

Vocabulary

1. camping
2. desert
3. wildlife
4. cliffs
5. forests
6. disappointing
7. coast
8. Canyon
9. mountains
10. skyscrapers
11. attraction
12. tourist

Unit 10

Grammar

B *Possible answers*

have to have / has to play / has to play / has to show / doesn't have to show / has to include / should have / should cost / don't have to cost / should look for / doesn't have to be

C *Answers will vary.*

Listening

makers / online / work / creamy / coffee / clean / salt / batteries / freezer / summer / crazy

Vocabulary

Across
1. electronic
2. scissors
3. gadget
4. headphones
5. warranty
6. microwave oven
7. battery
8. still photos
9. digital
10. hard drive
11. compact

Down
12. lightweight

Unit 11

Grammar

B *Questions*
1. Do you know what animals are endangered?
2. Can you tell me what environmental problems you have?
3. Do you know what laws protect the environment?
4. Do you understand why some people don't care about the environment?
5. Can you tell me how we can protect endangered species?

Possible answers
1. I don't know what animals are endangered.
2. I'm not sure what environmental problems we have.
3. I have no idea what laws protect the environment.
4. I don't understand why some people don't care about the environment.
5. I'm not sure how we can protect endangered species.

C *Answers will vary.*

Listening

countries / forests / scientists / species / medicinal / cancer / medicines / flower / cures / destroyed / 50

Vocabulary

Across
2. endangered
4. captivity
7. extinct
8. predator
10. wild
11. recycle
12. mammals

Down
1. protect
3. insects
5. repair
6. reptiles
9. pets

Unit 12

Grammar

B 1. Last / while / While / when / later / When *or* After / ago / Then / yesterday
2. ago / When / When *or* After / later / last / later / while / when

C *Answers will vary.*

Listening

German / bicycle / 22 / stealing / later / free / helping / station / chased / friend / quickly

Vocabulary
1. headline
2. burglar
3. classifieds
4. search
5. election
6. Atlantic Ocean
7. magazine
8. honeymoon
9. rescue
10. competition
11. trophy
12. Internet
13. happy ending

Unit 13

Grammar

B 1. Please turn your cell phone off / turn off your cell phone.
2. We don't want to wake up the children / wake the children up.
3. If he's very late, I'm not going to wait for my friend.
4. We usually get around the city by bus or subway.
5. I often call up my parents / call my parents up on the weekend.
6. Can you tell me how to plug in my laptop / plug my laptop in?

C *Questions*
1. When you turn a light on, do you always turn it off?
2. When you receive a letter in the mail, do you cut it open?
3. When you go out with a friend, what do you like to do?
4. Do you recycle old newspapers and magazines, or do you throw them out?
5. When people leave you a message, do you call them back right away?

Answers will vary.

Listening

parents / friendly / stranger / especially / downtown / safe / neighborhood / town / entertainment / museums / knowing

Vocabulary
1. conditioner
2. confused
3. country
4. stranger
5. cautious
6. jewelry
7. inside
8. wallet
9. unlocked
10. shoplifter
11. mugger
12. robber

```
C K C O N F U S E D Y A
B O M U G G E R S C J C
U R Y A V O T N T O J C
R O B B E R Y B R N C A
C A U T I O U S A D O U
B P L V C K R K N I U N
Y A K U R S A N G T N L
C L W A L L E T E I T O
N A E T Y B R B R O R C
L C J E W E L R Y N Y K
U E O L O B B V E E S E
A Y T I N S I D E R T D
T S H O P L I F T E R L
U S Y O U S U J J L U U
```

Unit 14

Grammar

B 1. one / enjoys / Each / has / One / is / both / feel / Neither / likes / both / love

2. None / is / each / likes / Some / like / some / enjoy / some / love / all / do / All / have

C *Answers will vary.*

Listening
romantic / falling / worst / action / thrilled / discussions / problems / surprised / feelings / hating / boyfriend

Vocabulary
Across
1. artistic
2. theater
3. classical music
4. special effects
5. posters
6. quotes
7. background
8. easy listening
9. favorite
10. jazz
11. paintings
12. director

Down
13. self-portrait

Unit 15
Grammar
B was designed / was named / was murdered / were met / was shot / were destroyed / were organized / were killed

C *Possible answers*
1. The Berlin Wall was taken down by the Germans in 1989.
2. The church of Hagia Sophia was built by Emperor Justinian in the 6th century.
3. Many people were killed by a tsunami in the Indian Ocean in 2004.
4. The people of the United States were given the Statue of Liberty by France in 1876.
5. The city of New Orleans was destroyed by Hurricane Katrina in 2005.
6. The Taj Mahal was built by an Indian prince in the 17th century.

Listening
Guide 1: Bridge / 1894 / 18 / one / grandsons / granddaughter
Guide 2: cathedral / 1804 / 1812 / 1815 / 51

Vocabulary
Across
2. guide
3. date
8. lifetime
9. statue
11. century
12. changed
Down
1. temple
4. event
5. childhood
6. historical
7. building
10. memory

Unit 16
Grammar
B 1. *Saturday Night Live* is an American comedy show that / which began in 1975.
2. SNL is a popular program that / which is watched by millions of people every week.
3. There are many famous comedians who / that started their careers on SNL.
4. The show is famous for its hilarious parodies that / which make fun of celebrities.
5. A favorite SNL character was a little girl who / that jumped on her bed and sang.
6. Will Ferrell and Adam Sandler are two actors who / that became famous on SNL.
7. There are comedy shows all over the world that / which were inspired by SNL.
8. Steve Martin is an actor who / that has hosted the show 13 times.

C *Answers will vary.*

Listening
Jack: examined / three / green / blue / red
Mary: operation / hospital / nurse / simple / worry / comfort

Vocabulary
1. hilarious
2. slapstick
3. cartoon
4. joke
5. chuckle
6. giggle
7. funniest
8. comedy show
9. comedian
10. punch line
11. riddle
12. envelope

Acknowledgments

Illustration Credits

Carlos Castellanos: vi–vii, 10, 28, 33, 55, 73
Jim Haynes: 15, 60, 61
Kim Johnson: 2, 3, 40, 47, 71
William Waitzman: 23, 79, 87

Photo Credits

Cover ©Frank Veronsky
4 (*clockwise from top left*) ©Stephen Simpson/Getty Images; ©Steven Puetzer/Getty Images; ©Corbis; ©Stephen Johnson/Getty Images
5 ©Shutterstock
6 (*clockwise from top left*) ©Jupiter Images; ©Siri Stafford/Getty Images; ©Jupiter Images; ©Jupiter Images
8 (*left to right*) ©Jupiter Images; ©Jamey O'Quinn; ©Jupiter Images
9 ©Photos.com
11 ©Eyecandy Images/Alamy
12 (*left to right*) ©Anthony Johnson/Getty Images; ©Alamy; ©Jupiter Images
13 (*top*) ©Envision/Corbis; (*bottom, both*) ©Punchstock
16 (*clockwise from top left*) ©Robert Holmes/Alamy; ©Richard Chung/Reuters/Landov; ©Gala/SuperStock; ©Jose Luis Pelaez/Corbis
17 (*window frames*) ©Alamy; (*skies*) ©Shutterstock
18 (*left to right*) ©Joel Nito/AFP/Getty Images; ©Stan Honda/AFP/Getty Images; ©Peter Holst/Getty Images
19 (*top to bottom*) ©Douglas Walker/Getty Images; ©Veer/Dale O'Dell/Getty Images
22 (*top, clockwise from top left*) ©Zigy Kaluzny/Getty Images; ©Charles Gupton/Getty Images; ©Alamy; ©Transtock Inc./Alamy; (*bottom*) ©Alex Mares-Manton/Jupiter Images
24 (*clockwise from top left*) ©Leo Jones; ©AFP/Getty Images; ©Warner Independent/Everett; ©Dean Conger/Corbis
26 (*clockwise from top left*) ©Punchstock; ©Andrea Booher/Getty Images; ©Corbis; ©Getty Images
27 (*clockwise from top left*) ©Punchstock; ©Jamie Grill/Getty Images; ©Darius Ramazani/Zefa/Corbis; ©Phil Boorman/Getty Images; ©Punchstock; ©Leland Bobbé/Corbis
29 (*top to bottom*) ©Punchstock; ©Jupiter Images; ©Andrew Hobbs/Getty Images
30 (*left to right*) ©Armando Franca/AP/Wide World; ©Jupiter Images; ©AFP/Getty Images
32 (*clockwise from top left*) ©Bill Aron/PhotoEdit; ©Alamy; ©AP/Wide World; ©Jupiter Images; ©Alamy; ©Jupiter Images
34 (*left to right*) ©Carlos Barria/Reuters/Corbis; ©Jeremy Horner/Corbis; ©Daly&Newton/Getty Images
35 (*left to right*) ©Photos.com; ©Alamy; ©Jupiter Images; ©Jupiter Images; ©Istock
36 (*left to right*) ©Walter Bibikow/Getty Images; ©Qilai Shen/EPA/Corbis; ©Chip Porter/Getty Images
37 (*left to right*) ©Jupiter Images; ©Jesco Tscholitsch/Getty Images; ©Jason Hetherington/Getty Images
41 (*clockwise from top left*) ©Jupiter Images; ©Corbis; ©Jupiter Images; ©Koji Aoki/Jupiter Images
42 (*clockwise from top left*) ©Isifa Image Service/Alamy; ©Jon Arnold Images/Alamy; ©Look Die Bildagentur der Fotografen/Alamy; ©Imagebroker/Alamy; ©Vario Images/Alamy
43 (*left to right*) ©Travel Pix/Getty Images; ©Stephen Frink/Getty Images
44 (*clockwise from top*) ©Shutterstock; ©Alamy; ©Kyodo/Landov; ©Alamy; ©Alamy; ©Shutterstock
45 (*both*) ©Shutterstock
46 (*top three rows, all*) ©Shutterstock; (*bottom, left to right*) ©Courtesy of Machina, Inc.; ©Courtesy of The Safety Zone; ©Courtesy of Vitra Products

48 (*left to right*) ©John Sturrock/Alamy; ©Tony Anderson/Getty Images; ©Jupiter Images
49 (*left to right*) ©Nigel J. Dennis/Gallo Images/Corbis; ©Keren Su/China Span/Alamy
50 (*left to right*) ©Punchstock; ©Jorge Saenz/AP/Wide World; ©SuperStock
51 ©Macduff Everton/Getty Images
52 (*clockwise from top left*) ©George Frey/Getty Images; ©Gibsons of Scilly; ©Bill Alkofer/ Corbis; ©Jonathan Ernst/Reuters/Landov
53 (*clockwise from top left*) ©John Lund/Getty Images; ©Terje Rakke/Getty Images; ©Stephanie Reix/Corbis; ©AP/Wide World
54 ©Shutterstock
58 (*left to right*) ©Liu Xiaoyang/Alamy; ©Alamy
59 (*left to right*) ©SuperStock; ©Kim Karpeles/Alamy; ©Tibor Bognar/Alamy
60 ©Shutterstock
62 (*clockwise from top left*) ©Jose Luis Pelaez/Corbis; ©Antony Nagelmann/Getty Images; ©SuperStock; ©Mango Productions/Corbis; ©Jupiter Images; ©Punchstock
63 (*top to bottom*) ©Pictorial Press/Alamy; ©Miramax/Everett; ©New Line/Picture Desk
64 (*clockwise from top left*) ©Bettmann/Corbis; ©Shutterstock; ©Manfred Rutz/Getty Images; ©SuperStock; ©Art Resource; ©Peter Horree/Alamy
65 (*left to right*) ©Amanda Hall/Getty Images; ©Courtesy estate of MC Escher; ©Richard Cummins/SuperStock
66 (*both*) ©George Kerrigan
67 (*left to right*) ©Henry Diltz/Corbis; ©Jasper James/Getty Images; ©Jupiter Images
68 (*clockwise from top left*) ©Free Agents Limited/Corbis; ©Steve Vidler/SuperStock; ©Janet Wishnetsky/Corbis; ©Francesco Venturi/Corbis; ©Steve Vidler/Estock; ©Siegfried Layda/Getty Images; ©Darby Sawchuk/Alamy; ©Yann Layma/Getty Images
70 (*clockwise from top left*) ©Stephen Swintek/Getty Images; ©George Caswell/Jupiter Images; ©Robin Bartholick/Punchstock; ©Miramax/Everett; ©MGM/Everett; ©ITV/Rex Features/Everett
72 (*clockwise from top left*) ©Cartoonbank; ©Cartoonbank; ©Cartoonstock; ©Cartoonstock; ©Cartoonstock
77 ©George Kerrigan
78 (*top to bottom*) ©Carlos Sanchez Pereyra/Estock; ©Jupiter Images; ©Punchstock
80 (*top, left to right*) ©Courtesy of Panasonic; ©Courtesy of UCO Play and Freeze; (*bottom, top to bottom*) ©Alamy; ©Punchstock; ©Cliff LeSergent/Alamy; ©Alamy
81 (*clockwise from top*) ©Joel Sartore/Getty Images; ©Jupiter Images; ©Michael Gottschalk/Getty Images
82 (*left to right*) ©Paul Almassy/Corbis; ©Andy Warhol Foundation/Corbis
85 ©George Kerrigan
86 (*top to bottom*) ©Michele Falzone/Alamy; ©Michael S. Yamashita/Corbis; ©Jupiter Images
88 (*top, left to right*) ©Courtesy of Panasonic; ©Courtesy of UCO Play and Freeze; (*bottom, top to bottom*) ©Alamy; ©Punchstock; ©Cliff LeSergent/Alamy; ©Alamy
89 (*clockwise from top*) ©Michael Gottschalk/Getty Images; ©Joel Sartore/Getty Images; ©Jupiter Images
90 (*left to right*) ©Paul Almassy/Corbis; ©Andy Warhol Foundation/Corbis
91 (*clockwise from top*) ©Jupiter Images; ©Michael Gottschalk/Getty Images; ©Joel Sartore/Getty Images